WHERE THERE'S A WILL...

*A Guide for the Executor or Administrator
of the Estate of a Decedent*

by F. William Bauers, Jr.

Disclaimer

This book contains useful and accurate information concerning the subject matter. Be aware that laws and procedures constantly change and are subject to different interpretations. This book is not intended to be used as a substitute for seeking expert advice and the contents of this publication should not be construed as legal advice. If legal advice or other expert assistance is required, the services of a competent professional should be sought.. The publisher and author are not engaged in rendering legal, tax, accounting or other professional service.

Dedicated to the love of my life, Joanne Turney Bauers, who inspired me to write this book and offered encouragement along the way.

About The Author

F. William Bauers, Jr. grew up in San Antonio, Texas and holds both a B.A. and an MBA from the George Washington University. He has been a Partner in a firm engaged in management counsel; Senior Vice President of a building and development firm; Vice President and General Manager of an international real estate firm; and President of his own firm. He presently manages four trusts. He divides his time between New York City, Swarthmore, PA, and Washington D.C.

Acknowledgments

This is to recognize with appreciation and gratitude those friends who reviewed my manuscript and made both editorial and substantive contributions.

Gant Redmon, Esq., Managing Partner, Redmon, Boykin and Braswell, L.L.P., Attorneys at Law

Stephen J. McGann, Trust Officer, First National Bank of West Chester

Clayton E. Cameron, Cameron & Associates, P.C., CPA's

George Alexander, Publishing Consultant

Edmund Jones, Esq., Jones, Guthrie & Strohm, Attorneys at Law

The Reverend Dr. Mark S. Anschutz, Rector, St. Michael and All Angels Church

Michael A. Doyle, Editor and Layout Design

I deeply appreciate their support and professional assistance.

Foreward

Being lost on a footpath in the woods, on the streets of a strange city or on an unfamiliar highway will convince you of the benefit of having a compass, a guide, or a good map. Guidance helps to remove the uncertainty and contributes to a relaxing journey and timely arrival at your destination.

If you have been designated as an executor, expect to be, or want a better understanding of the process, I recommend *Where There's a Will...* This book provides direction and guidance for the executor, who is the person designated to carry out the wishes of the testator, and to administer his or her estate - that is, to discharge liabilities and to distribute the assets. As the title implies, this book is intended primarily for one named in a document prepared by or for the deceased, but for one appointed as administrator of an estate where there is no will, much of the information is equally applicable. The principal distinction is that distribution would be determined by applicable state law rather than as expressed in a will.

Having accompanied the author on some of the major journeys described in the text, serving as legal counsel, I can assure you that he has drawn from practical experience as an executor in the U. S. and abroad and from the wisdom gained in facing complex problems and issues. The guidance this book provides will be of significant assistance to you in facing similar issues and fulfilling the responsibilities of the executor.

The knowledge that you will gain will make your service as an executor or administrator more rewarding and enable you to take more timely and effective action, from initial qualification to final distribution and accounting. *Where There's a Will...* is designed to serve as both a reference and guide. The duties of the executor are outlined in Chapter 3, and more complete information relating to each duty is described in a referenced chapter of the book. The author has used a narrative style to relate some of the relevant and interesting situations in which he was involved as executor in various states of the U.S. and several European countries. He also has provided detailed information in the text, and sample letters and forms in the Appendix to guide you in what to do, how to do it and when it will be expected of you. The Case studies illustrate the principles and problems described and solutions reached.

While the processes and functions dealt with in this work are not likely to change in the foreseeable future, the specific laws under which you will function frequently do change. For example, the District of Columbia recently updated its probate code. It is therefore desirable to secure as one of your initial actions a copy of the applicable law and court rules, including the schedule of filings required by the court administering probate. Sample forms and filings are included in the Appendix.

Where There's a Will... is intended to provide the direction helpful in carrying out the intent of the testator, discharging your responsibility as executor and honoring the trust bestowed upon you. The presentation is one that you will find quite interesting.

It has been my honor to have a long professional and personal relationship with the author and with his family. I am delighted that he has chosen to share his experience in order to assist others who serve as executors or administrators or as counsel.

Gant Redmon, Managing Partner
Redmon, Boykin & Braswell, L.L.P.
Alexandria, Virginia

TABLE OF CONTENTS

INTRODUCTION

If you were advised that your uncle had just died suddenly and you were named as his Executor, would you know what to do, or where to begin? Most of us have not served as an executor and have little knowledge of the role, yet it is a role that most of us will be exposed to at some point. We are likely to serve as executor of the estate of a family member or to be affected by the process. We need to understand what is involved. When one is abruptly required to act and has no time for study or reflection it is important to have knowledge of what to do.

Having served as an executor a number of times and based upon conversations with family members, relatives, friends and acquaintances, I concluded that there is a need for a guide for the lay executor. This guide is based primarily upon my experience as an executor and trustee, business background and education, but also on the knowledge that I have gained from many hours of discussions with attorneys, insurance brokers, account executives with stock brokerage firms, trust officers, bankers and financial planners. The presentation is designed to give an overall picture of what is involved in serving as an executor, to provide specific guidance on each aspect of the process, and to conclude with actual case studies. The Appendix includes forms and form letters which may be used by the executor. The events on which this work is based were actual occurrences. For obvious reasons some names were changed or omitted to protect the privacy of those involved.

As a lay executor one is likely to have professional assistance, and my belief is that the guidance and counsel of an attorney is essential, yet there is much that can and should be done independently. An attorney cannot be constantly at the executor's side for the year or more which may be required to settle an estate. Further, by knowing what is involved one can have a better understanding of the process and make more effective use of professional counsel. The intent is to provide simple basic knowledge and guidance for the lay person. The professional who serves as an executor or who assists clients also may find this book useful and may provide it to his clients. By sharing my experiences as an executor I want to provide a concept of what may be encountered and illustrate certain points. Specific requirements will vary because of differences in estates, documents existing, legal jurisdiction and requirements, but in much of the activity there is a common thread and similar requirement for action.

Serving as an executor, while presenting difficulties, is also an illuminating experience. Interesting things happen; travel may lead to unexpected adventure and intrigue; different aspects of personality are often revealed. There is an opportunity to learn as well as to serve the departed and the beneficiaries. My intent is to assist you who will bear the responsibility for administering the affairs of one who placed faith and trust in you, to help you to be better prepared for the task, and to provide guidance and a source of reference.

Chapter *One*

ON BEING AN EXECUTOR

The Bell Tolls

The jarring sound of the telephone ringing at one o'clock in the morning brought me out of a deep sleep. With trepidation I answered, having the feeling that it is usually bad news that comes in the middle of the night. The call came from California, three time zones away and across the continent from metropolitan Washington D.C., more specifically northern Virginia, where I was located. Uncle Arthur was calling to say that his brother Edward had died suddenly of a heart attack following dinner at his hotel in Torino, Italy. Edward had just started a two week vacation and was enroute to Portofino, on the Italian Riviera di Levante.

My Designation as an Executor

A short time prior to his death Edward had visited us at our home in Alexandria, Virginia and at that time he asked me to serve as his executor. My response, in effect, was "Why me?" Edward was a successful business executive working in Europe, representing a U.S. company. Why not an attorney, a bank, or a family member? I had worked with Edward in New York City before he moved to London. We had been partners in a firm engaged in Management Counsel and I suppose he felt he knew me and my capabilities. He had separated from his wife and as a result of the separation he was estranged from his wife's son. He had no children. Edward said in effect, "You are the only one whom I trust and I want you to serve in this capacity." It was difficult for me to decline, so I accepted, not having an inkling of where that decision would lead.

Abrupt End of a Vacation

Edward told me at the time I agreed to act as his executor that he would have his Will changed accordingly, and during his upcoming vacation in Italy he would write instructions regarding his wishes and send me a copy of his Will along with these instructions. My knowledge of his personal and financial affairs was very limited. Edward was 62 at the time and in relatively good health so I assumed there was no urgency, and he had promised to send me necessary data. So I was not concerned. Unfortunately Edward died in Torino on the first day of his vacation, having sent no information!

The Remains of the Day

My first thought after coming more fully awake was, "What do I do with the body of the deceased across the Atlantic in Italy?" I knew nothing of his desires as to a funeral or of how to proceed in a foreign country. Fortunately for me, Arthur had received the news in a call from Edward's secretary in London, who had read his Will. She stated that Edward had expressed his desire to be cremated and interred in California with his parents. Arthur said that Edward had wanted him to take care of the funeral arrangements. That took care of my first problem - or so I thought at the time.

Italy, a predominantly Roman Catholic country, was not in favor of cremation and there were few facilities available to perform the function. The problems of clearance for the remains to leave the country and arrangements for transportation also confronted me. With help from the Department of State, inasmuch as I was in the Washington, D. C. area, and from the U.S. Embassy in Rome, the necessary contacts were reached, and decisions made. The ashes were to be flown from Italy to New York and Edward's stepson was to accompany the remains from New York to California. Arthur made the arrangements for the funeral and interment in California. With these difficult arrangements completed I turned my attention to my new responsibilities as executor of the estate.

Where There's a Will

The first hurdle was past, but that was just the beginning. Edward, prior to his move to Europe, had been a resident of New York, although he was born in California. He was working in Europe as Vice President, European Operations, for a U.S. company which was based in Illinois. He had a flat (apartment) in London where he was residing and also had a flat in Brussels, Belgium. He was married but separated from his wife and not divorced. He died in Italy. At that point I decided I needed an attorney with rather broad experience who could work closely with me. I decided to engage an attorney who was an acquaintance and neighbor, who had gained some international exposure and who used a pragmatic approach to the law. Within a few weeks we were flying to London. But first I had to obtain the power to act as executor and I couldn't do that without the *will*. After several more international phone calls and some delay, Edward's secretary in London was persuaded to send the will (copied before mailing, and sent certified, registered or carrier). We reviewed the document, and filed it with the appropriate court requesting the authority for me to act - which is issued in the form of *Letters Testamentary*. We updated our passports, made travel arrangements - and we were on our way across the Atlantic to Europe. London seemed the logical starting point as Edward had been residing in London and his personal files were there. We landed at Heathrow and took a cab to his flat in Mayfair.

The High Cost of Delay

During this interim period of waiting for the will to be received from London and for probate, while I had neither authority nor power to act as executor; the Dow Jones average dropped substantially. A high percentage of the market value was lost and this drop in market prices resulted in a major loss in the value of the estate's stock portfolio. Of course, I was not aware at that time of the effect of the market drop, having no knowledge of the estate's investment holdings. Even if I'd had such knowledge there was nothing that I could have done at that point because I had not yet been legally appointed as executor and could not act.

Lesson One - Ask for the Facts

This brings us to the first lesson for the executor. Should you be asked to serve as an executor, insist upon obtaining as soon as possible complete information concerning the affairs of the person who is requesting you to serve, and the location of important documents. Most important are the **will,** any **trust documents,** and **instructions** from the person designating you regarding the administration of the estate. These needs will be discussed later in the text along with detailed information, summaries and check lists of what is desirable and or necessary for you to have.

The Mayfair Blockade

To return to London, one of the duties of an executor is to **collect the assets** of the decedent and to safeguard them. Edward had a leased flat in London's Mayfair which was also his London office. He owned the furnishings and art work in the apartment. On arrival in London we went immediately to the flat, only to find that it had been "sealed" by the U.S. Embassy in London. Ribbons were placed across the door and it was marked - **"Do Not Enter."** After inquiry we learned that if a U.S. citizen had been residing in a foreign country at the time of his death, typically the U.S. Embassy or Consulate will take charge of and inventory the assets of the decedent and protect them pending arrival of a family member or other authorized person. After presenting evidence of my authority - letters testamentary and a death certificate - and accepting responsibility for the contents of the flat, I was authorized entry and possession.

A Numbered Account

Edward's secretary, whom I will call Vi, came to the flat to review with us his papers and to pass on to us her limited knowledge of his financial affairs. The flat in Brussels was provided by and largely furnished by his employer. Edward had a Swiss numbered account with Bank Leu in Zurich. He had taken with him to Torino some of his personal papers (in order to prepare his instructions to me). He also had with him some confidential business papers regarding current company activities, which his employer was most anxious to obtain. There was very little information in London to assist me.

The London Flat

It was necessary to determine the appropriate disposition of the flat, and of the furnishings, artwork, clothing, personal papers and documents. To sublet the flat required the services of a London attorney and a leasing agent. The new tenant was obliged to pay *key money* to take over the flat. Key money was standard practice in London, a fee paid to assume the lease on a desirable flat, as they were in short supply. The prospective tenant offered *1500* and I insisted on *2000*. On settling I found that he was thinking British pounds and I was thinking U.S. dollars. So the estate came out ahead of my expectations on this transaction. We shipped the furniture to the U.S. as we couldn't sell it in London - there was no interest in Scandinavian modern. The clothing was sent to Edward's stepson; paintings and other items were also shipped for later sale or auction in the U.S. We conferred with a London accounting firm regarding tax liabilities in England and filing necessary forms.

A Problem in Brussels

Having completed all that we could accomplish in London, we flew to Brussels, Belgium, where Edward had an office and apartment. Brussels yielded no information concerning personal affairs and presented one big problem. On arrival at the apartment in Brussels we found it empty! After coming down from orbit, I called the U.S. Embassy in Brussels and ultimately spoke with a woman who had knowledge of the circumstances. She advised that the property of a deceased American is collected for protection. I told her that the Embassy had no authority to remove the property and demanded its immediate return. The Embassy spokesman didn't give a satisfactory response to my question as to why they had not just sealed the apartment, as in London. Instead she asked, "How am I supposed to get the estate property back there?" My answer was, "presumably in the same manner you transported it from the apartment to the Embassy warehouse." Within a day the furnishings, clothing, paintings and personal items were returned by truck and dumped unceremoniously in one big pile in the middle of the living room. It was then a major effort to sort out these belongings and arrange for their disposition. The flat was leased by the company which also had provided most of the furnishings. Thus after we obtained an inventory from the company, we released the flat and company-owned furnishings to an official of the company. The tangible personal property was shipped to the U.S., to the designated beneficiaries, again arranged through a shipping agent.

The Zurich Connection

Having completed the exhausting task of emptying the two flats and searching for information which did not make itself available, we flew to Zurich, Switzerland. Vi was aware of Edward's numbered account with Bank Leu but had not been able to elicit any information from the Bank in Zurich by telephone. Because of the Swiss secrecy laws concerning numbered accounts, I expected a problem in getting information from the Bank, but it was not a problem. The bank officials were polite and cooperative and after reviewing the letters testamentary, gave me the information concerning the bank account and the securities account which the Bank managed. I had mentioned that my maternal grandmother and ancestors were from Zurich. The banker recognized the family name and the name of their home, the Seidenhof, which he said had been torn down in the name of "progress." A room from the Seidenhof is in a museum in Zurich. This Zurich connection helped me to establish rapport with the bank officers. The account was closed and the funds and securities were transferred to the U.S.

A Limo in Torino

After a short stay in Zurich, we flew to Torino, Italy to interview local and State Department (Consular) officials, as well as employees at the hotel where Edward had been staying. Our arrival in Torino from the airport was widely noted as we were in a Mercedes 600 with driver. Having struggled into small European cars, we had asked for a large car, large enough to transport us and our baggage. This car was **LARGE**. It looked like we were conducting *Family* business. We endeavored to obtain more specific information as to the circumstances and cause of death, and to collect personal files and belongings. We also interviewed an employee of the Illinois company which had a consulting relationship with manufacturing companies in Torino. The company had, with my consent, retrieved the company papers prior to my arrival, based upon their expression of urgency of need and of confidentiality. We were not totally satisfied with the information we received from interviews and believed that our image resulting from the Mercedes influenced the result. We suspected foul play but that is another story. There were a few notes in the personal files but nothing of major assistance.

Torino is a charming city surrounded by lakes. I was impressed by the many sidewalks in the business district which were marble and covered overhead. The hotel was attractive and a stay of longer duration would have been pleasing. At that point, however, three weeks had elapsed since we had left the U.S. It was necessary to return to the U.S. in order to retain our regular employment as well as to proceed with the work of the executor.

Chapter *Two*

DESIGNATION AND RESPONSIBILITIES

Acceptance

Designation as an executor is likely to come to most of us - designation in the will of a spouse, perhaps other family member, relative, friend or business associate. Such designation is an honor as it indicates trust and confidence and the belief that you have the ability to perform, but *don't* get carried away by the honor! Performing as an executor can be a time consuming and difficult experience as evidenced by the first chapter. Much depends upon the complexity of the estate and the personalities of family members and beneficiaries - which I might add are not always one and the same.

The writer of a will, the "prospective decedent" or testator, when preparing a will has a choice in the selection or designation of an executor. The executor selected may be one or more individuals, an attorney, a corporate executor such as a bank, trust company or institution, or a combination. Those selected should be asked to serve and to accept and then should be provided with complete information in order to facilitate the completion of the task. Of course, this does not have to include personal information which the testator may not want to reveal at that time, such as net worth, amounts of bequests or beneficiaries. But do not accept an appointment lightly. Find out if you can what is involved prior to accepting and learn about the responsibilities beforehand.

Responsibilities

These responsibilities can include the operation of a business until it is disposed of, managing a stock and bond portfolio, determining what to sell and what to hold, selling real estate, selling antiques and works of art, providing income for beneficiaries, establishing trusts, working with professionals - accountants and attorneys, stock brokers, real estate brokers, trust officers, bankers and court officials, and last but not least - federal and state tax collectors. I don't mean to discourage acceptance, as serving can be a rewarding experience and not all estates are difficult or complex. Serving can be challenging but an understanding of what is involved and what to do can make the task infinitely more agreeable.

Qualification

In the case illustrated in Chapter One, Edward had appointed me as *co-executor* and *trustee* along with a major New York Bank Trust Department. There were several problems. The first was that I had no knowledge that he had named a co-executor. The will had been written by a law firm in New York State and called for probate in that state. I was not a resident of New York and not blood related to the decedent; therefore, I could not serve in New York. The bank had not been contacted for agreement to serve. The bank policy was not to serve as co-executor; the bank was to be sole executor, or nothing; and further, the estate did not meet their financial criteria. These policies prevented the bank from serving. Because they had been named in a legal document, however, it was necessary for me to petition the bank to withdraw, and for the bank to concur. The whole effort involved was wearing, disconcerting and time consuming. Time lost often proves to be expensive, as it did in this case.

If you are asked to serve as an executor and you agree, it should be ascertained that you are legally qualified to do so according to the laws of the State, and that the co-executor, if any, also is so qualified. Otherwise, you may have a problem. In the instance related it was necessary to probate the estate in the jurisdiction in which I, now the sole executor and trustee, then resided - the Commonwealth of Virginia. Since the domicile of the deceased was not clear and as I could not serve in New York, the decedent on the advice of counsel became domiciled in Virginia - at least we made the determination that it had been his intent to reside there.

The Need to Know

As a prospective executor, try to obtain as complete a knowledge as you can of the type of assets involved in the estate; for example, real property, bank and savings accounts, stock brokerage accounts, limited partnerships, partnerships, companies owned or operated, and tangible personal property. It would be helpful to know the location of activities and properties, persons to be contacted, the value of various assets and their intended disposition, buy and sell agreements and insurance carried - life, health and other.

Of course, you may not learn that you are the executor, until after the fact, when it is too late to ask questions. Then you may have to spend a great deal of time and energy ferreting out the location of information, assets and amounts involved, and determining what to do with what you have, or you may decline to serve. An alternate or a court appointed executor would then serve in your stead.

Fiduciary Position

As an executor you occupy a *fiduciary* position, a position of trust, which is governed by law. Your responsibility is to gather the assets, safeguard them, and consolidate them, and to administer the estate as required by the last will and testament, any trust agreements and the law. At death any revocable trust becomes irrevocable and the assets in the trust are governed by the trust agreement. What you do with the assets governed by the will and any other valid legal documents signed by the decedent will be determined by those documents and the probate court. In a simple estate - if any are simple - you may be required to sell the assets or to distribute them according to the will. The sale of a house and or a car may be involved. In a more complex situation, the estate stock portfolio may hold speculative or volatile issues subject to wide swings in market price. As a fiduciary you cannot continue to hold such stocks in a portfolio as a substantial loss could occur if the market declines or a particular stock suddenly drops in market value. What you do is a matter of judgment, governed by prudence, fiduciary responsibility and legal authority and restrictions. You may be liable if you fail to act or if you are negligent or act improperly.

Payment of Taxes

As executor you are responsible for the payment of Federal and State Income Taxes to the date of death of the decedent, and for the payment of Federal Estate Taxes and State Inheritance Taxes. Federal Estate Tax Returns are due nine months after the date of death along with payment of the taxes due, and State Inheritance Tax Returns are due as specified. If insufficient cash is available for payment of taxes you may have to sell assets. Do not distribute funds, other than essential income to beneficiaries, make bequests or discharge other than required debt payments until you have ascertained that there are adequate funds available for payment of taxes. If sufficient assets were available at the time of death and they are no longer available, you the executor could be required personally to make the payment of taxes. Tax liabilities **must** be satisfied.

Personal Property

Personal property distribution can cause major problems. First, a distinction has to be made between *personal effects* and *tangible personal property*. They are not necessarily one and the same and legally may be treated in a different manner. In one instance in which I was the executor, the decedent's "tangible personal property" was left by will to one beneficiary along with separate handwritten instructions as to the wishes of the decedent for the disposition of china, silver, jewelry, certain pieces of furniture, and collections of art objects. The beneficiary consulted an attorney as to what constitutes "tangible personal property." It was the Texas attorney's opinion that tangible personal property included *savings accounts*. This beneficiary, who had signatory authority on the accounts, but not joint ownership, withdrew the funds. The savings accounts were principal assets of the estate. This left the executor with no funds for payment of funeral expenses, administration expenses, or taxes. After a heated discussion the beneficiary agreed to return the funds. Other Attorneys fail to agree that the attorney who was consulted by the beneficiary was correct. In any case it was clearly the intent of the decedent to distribute the estate equally between her three children, as she and her husband had agreed, and this desire was fulfilled. Nevertheless, a major problem grew out of error in drawing up the will, which should have stated **personal effects** rather than **tangible personal property**. Further, this beneficiary declined to distribute the personal effects as specified because her attorney said separate handwritten instructions were not "legally binding." However, holographic codicils may be binding.

A Cause of Conflict

Disputes often arise over items which are not of importance from a monetary value but which have value to the beneficiaries or heirs and are not specifically designated as to who should receive them. These items might be a particular piece of jewelry, furniture, or an art object. In one instance season tickets for the New York Football Giants were claimed by three different entities causing a major confrontation at the Giant's stadium at a football game when two entities endeavored to use the seats at the time. One had the tickets, the other the presumed legal right. The question of ownership of these tickets created a major headache for me, the executor.

It is advisable to have a list of those things, personal effects, which may be coveted or desired by more than one individual, included in the Will with indication of the intended recipient. The list could be a codicil to an existing will. Making such a list is time consuming and it forces one to consider one's demise in a more personal way than other aspects of a will might, so it is easy to procrastinate. A list written separately from a will might be ignored if the responsible person involved elects to do so. Such a list may be considered not legally binding, although in my opinion it is morally binding. If you are consulted in advance by the testator you might recommend consideration of the disposition of personal effects with a list of items and intended recipients specified in the will. It might prevent a battle, save refereeing or avoid a rift between family members, or other beneficiaries.

Information Needs

To get to the more mundane, a vast amount of time can be consumed in trying to find information which was not provided by the departed. For example, you are likely to need identification numbers of the decedent including social security, driver's license, passport, military serial or service numbers and VA claim numbers, and the names of family members and friends, their telephone numbers, and organizational memberships, club memberships, licenses, bank and savings accounts and location, etc. It is relatively easy for the living to develop such information and to make it available. The executor really doesn't have the time to wade through files or search for information while making funeral arrangements, looking after the family, solving immediate problems and taking care of urgent matters.

Considerations

All that has been said up to this point should have convinced you that if you are named as an executor you need to have a serious talk with yourself and with the testator so that you may know at least in part what to anticipate. You may have an input or influence using your newly found knowledge after reading this treatise, to make it easier for yourself down the road. If you were appointed as executor and not notified in advance that you were, good luck! The level of difficulty is increased.

If everything was set up properly by the decedent your task can be relatively simple but not necessarily without conflict. My mother, for example, did notify me in advance of my designation as executor and also made my task easier by preplanning her funeral, filing all the necessary personal affairs documents together in one file, showing me the location of the file and giving me a copy of her will in advance. The will directed that her home be sold, so there was no discussion on that point. The beneficiaries had the opportunity to purchase the home at the appraised market value if they so chose. Such procedure is infinitely better than leaving the property by will to several beneficiaries. Multiple owners rarely agree as to the disposition of the property, the timing or the contract provisions, which makes a sale difficult. If a sale **is** made, delay in acceptance of a contract can be unacceptable to the buyer. Also, if the will directs the sale of property, title does not pass to the heirs. In my mother's case the house had to be sold. I had the power to sell it and the experience as a real estate broker to do so. So in this case, the disagreement with the beneficiaries centered on what repairs and improvements were to be made prior to sale, and whether to take a first trust from the purchaser. This was in a period of 16 per cent interest rates and difficulty in placing mortgages. As I had the complete authority, I did what I thought best. "Power corrupts and absolute power is really neat." (John Lehman). I accepted a first trust at below market interest for a five year term and sold the house in five days. The trust was paid off after two years.

What follows in this treatise is intended to assist you in the performance of your duties. As an executor you have important duties to perform. The decedent is no longer able to control his or her personal, business and financial affairs. You must act according to the direction of the decedent as expressed in the will and trust agreements and instructions, and according to the laws of competent jurisdiction.

Chapter *Three*

DUTIES OF THE EXECUTOR

What to Do

The executor has a number of duties and while it is possible to list these duties and to explain them in some order, it may be impossible to perform them in that order, or in any particular order. Some tasks will be performed concurrently and others will be performed sooner or later perhaps than they should have been. But if you as executor also are a family member, relative, close friend or associate of the deceased, you may not be performing completely up to par. Coping with the loss and concomitant emotions of shock, anger, disbelief, and grief reduces the level of performance. Other family members who may be in a state of shock have to be comforted and also persuaded to take certain actions. Although each decision may not be the best, it is necessary to act, and it is helpful to have things that must be taken care of to occupy your time and distract you. Completing necessary tasks provides satisfaction and confirms your competence to perform.

Duties of the executor are listed and explained briefly in this chapter. More detailed information is provided in the chapters which follow. This is a general guide which will help to determine what to do but specifics may vary. In one situation there may be no other family members and in others there are family members who will want to participate. The duties of the executor will vary. There are situations where the will is contested, some where the will has complex provisions, or some where the situation or the tax law has changed and the will is not current. Some wills call for establishing a testamentary trust or trusts. There may be existing revocable trusts. Revocable trusts become irrevocable upon death of the grantor. So while there are differences, there are enough similarities to make this list useful. Remember that in performing the duties of the executor the sequence will vary. Specific requirements will differ because of the differences in estates and the legal requirements based on the governing documents and legal jurisdiction.

How to Proceed - A List of Duties

1. Assume Responsibility as Executor. The executor needs to become involved as soon as possible to assist family members and take necessary actions, including safeguarding assets (see #9. below), although the executor has no legal authority until appointed by the court.

2. Look for the Will and related documents, including burial instructions. If you don't know the location of the will try personal affairs files, office files, the office of the decedent's attorney and the Safe Deposit Box or boxes. Note: in some jurisdictions the Safe Deposit Box will be sealed upon the death of the box holder and access will be governed by state law.

3. Review the documents that are available. Confer with a co-executor if one was named and with any fiduciaries named, such as an attorney or trust department. If no one was named you may want to contact the decedent's attorney or to select legal counsel.

4. Serve the terminally ill. Assist the family. Consult with the family if there is an advance directive, or living will, and provide a copy to the hospital. If anatomical bequests or organ donations were specified, discuss the provisions with the family and medical authorities. (See Chapter 4, The Final Days.)

5. Make funeral arrangements. Contact the Clergy and the funeral director. Obtain death certificates through the funeral home. Request 10 to 25 copies initially as required. Provide information for the death notice, write the obituary and submit it or provide information through the funeral director to the newspapers for publication. (See Chapter 5, Considerations at Time of Death.)

6. Call family members and friends. Consult family members and ask them who should be notified, and who they wish to make the calls. (See Chapter 6, Notifications.)

7. Obtain documents. After you obtain the original executed will, look for trust agreements and other necessary documents. Request Federal ID number for the estate from the attorney or IRS. (See Chapter 7, Obtaining Documentation.)

8. Arrange for probate. Apply to the Register of Wills, County Clerk or Probate Court to place the will on record and enter an order to admit for probate. (See Chapter 8, Probate, and Appendix.)

   a. Submit application for probate and file the will with death certificate

   b. Post notice as required, in the court and newspapers

   c. Obtain authority to act as executor, issued as *letters testamentary* or *letters of administration.*

9. Collect and safeguard assets (high priority) - provide immediate physical security and insurance as necessary for cash, jewelry, automobiles, real estate and business activities. (See Chapter 9, Collection, Inventory and Safeguarding Assets.)

Open a bank checking account in the name of the estate as a repository and an additional interest bearing account if appropriate.

10. Make Notifications to banks, savings & loan associations, credit card companies and organizations. (See Chapter 6, Notifications, and Appendix.)

11. Take Inventory of Assets and arrange for valuation or appraisal of assets for filing - real properties, autos, antiques, jewelry. (See Chapter 9, Collection, Inventory and Safeguarding Assets.)

12. Make a financial analysis of the estate - determine assets and liabilities, income sources, debts and expenses. (See Chapter 10, Financial Analysis.)

13. Provide for immediate family income. (See Chapter 11, Providing for Immediate Family Income and Business Needs.)

14. Collect income and accounts receivable. (See Chapter 12, Collection of Income and Accounts.)

15. Collect Insurance payable to the estate or to Trusts. (See Chapter 13, Collection of Insurance, and Appendix.)

16. Collect Benefits - employment and military. (See Chapter 14, Filing for Benefits.)

17. File inventory of assets and appraisals with court as required. (See Chapter 8, Probate, and Chapter 9, Collection, Inventory, Safeguarding of Assets.)

18. File Income Tax returns for the decedent, income to date of death. (See Chapter 15, Payment of Taxes) and for any previous year not filed.

19. File Federal Estate Tax and State Inheritance Tax forms and pay taxes. (See Chapter 15, Payment of Taxes, and Appendix.) File Estate income tax returns covering earnings for the period after decedent's death until estate closing, Form 1041 and K-1's.

20. Pay funeral expenses and other expenses and debts. (See Chapter 16, Payment of Debts.)

21. Pay Bequests as specified in the will. (See Chapter 17, Payment of Bequests, and Appendix.)

22. Transfer assets, arrange disposition. (See Chapter 18, Disposition of Assets.)

23. Sell Real Estate or Securities as specified or required. (See Chapter 18, Disposition of Assets.)

24. Prepare An Accounting of the Estate for Beneficiaries. (See Chapter 10, Financial Analysis, Estate Summary.)

25. Make Distributions of the Estate to Beneficiaries or Trusts in accordance with the Will. (See Chapter 19, Establishing Trusts.)

26. Establish Testamentary Trusts specified in the Will. (See Chapter 19.)

27. Obtain Tax clearance letter from IRS and close Estate. (See Chapter 15, Payment of Taxes and Chapter 20, Closing the Estate.)

Chapter *Four*

THE FINAL DAYS

Advance Directive

There may be a time when the person who selected you to serve as executor is considered to be terminal, or terminally ill, as the result of an accident, cancer or stroke or other illness. This is a most difficult time for the family yet there are things to be done. If an *Advance Directive* or *Living Will* has been signed and executed, a copy of the document should be provided for the attending physician and the hospital. This document reflects the wishes of the person who signed it regarding life-sustaining treatment in particular circumstances. The signer may request that such treatment be withheld if he or she as patient is in a terminal condition or state of permanent unconsciousness. If you or another person holds a durable power of attorney, it would permit decision making if the patient is unable to act in the absence of a living will.

Medical Treatment

With a living will medical treatment for the terminally ill may be limited to that which relieves pain. The signer of the living will or advance directive may reject cardiac resuscitation, mechanical respiration, and invasive forms of treatment. A person may have been designated as surrogate to make medical treatment decisions in specified situations. The living will should be signed voluntarily and witnessed by two persons who are **not** related to the signer. If the living will was witnessed by family members the document may not be accepted, thus thwarting the desires of the patient, resulting in additional and unrewarding medical expense, and prolonging the agony of all concerned. Living Wills may not be accepted in all states or localities but there is wider acceptance than in the past.

Organ Donation

The terminally ill patient may have elected to be an organ donor. Such election may be noted on the driver's license or in another document. If this election has been made, notification of attending medical personnel is of critical importance. In case of an accident the decision may have to be made regarding withdrawal of life support if there is a cessation of brain activity. Such a decision would have to made by the next of kin or person designated in an advance directive and medical authorities in accordance with the law, or by a person holding a durable power of attorney.

Autopsy

The question of an autopsy can be another difficult decision. An autopsy may be required by law, or requested by medical authorities to determine the cause of death or to further medical research. If you are a family member you may be involved in this decision. As a non-family member executor you can provide a shoulder to lean on or provide objective, concerned advice if requested.

Preplanning

During such a terminal period it is advisable to preplan funeral arrangements, to endeavor to locate pertinent documents and to notify distant family members of the situation and when their presence might be required. Hospice and hospital personnel and the clergy can be consulted for advice.

Difficulties Encountered

The final days of life of a family member are difficult for the family. If they are in a distant location they aren't sure of when their presence is required or of what to do when there. The question may arise as to use of "heroic" measures to sustain life if the patient is terminally ill, or whether to remove life support if the patient is in a coma and suffered permanent brain damage. The executor, if a family member, may be involved in the decision or with the support of those who are. There are no easy answers in most situations.

Chapter *Five*

CONSIDERATIONS AT TIME OF DEATH

Guidance

At the time of a death there are a myriad of things which must be done and it is difficult to know what to do first. Following a step by step process is suggested by the Reverend Dr. Mark S. Anschutz, who was Rector of the Church which I attended for a number of years, and I borrow heavily from his "Guide for Christian Burial." It is most useful, reflecting his experience from many years in ministry. Also included are some thoughts of my own. This guidance should be helpful regardless of religious persuasion. What is not pertinent may be disregarded. Decisions may be made by family members, by the executor if there is no family present, or perhaps jointly by friends. These suggestions are by necessity general because situations vary; make use of them as suits the particular situation.

What to Do

You may wish to proceed as follows:

1. Call your clergy, whose experience and concern will be helpful, and seek their assistance.

2. If the deceased had expressed wishes regarding the service, either orally or in a document to which you have access, follow this guidance if possible.

3. If an autopsy is requested determine whether the law may require it, or it serves a medical purpose or necessity or is in accordance with the wishes of the family.

4. The deceased may have elected donation of the body to medical science or cremation. Such election may be one the family does not want to follow. The next of kin may endeavor to over rule the election.

5. Select a funeral director, if one was not previously chosen, and ask the director to take the body into custody and to await further discussion as to plans.

6. Select the type of service desired and location where it is to be held, whether public or private, church and burial service, or memorial service. Select the date and time, allowing for those travelling from a distant location. Will service include the Holy Eucharist? What Psalms, Lessons, Prayers, Hymns?

7. Determine where burial is to take place - is there an owned cemetery plot? If so, who owns it and where is the record of ownership? If purchase of a plot is required, select the cemetery and size of plot. If there is a military burial , contact the Supervisor of the national cemetery and the office of the chaplain.

8. Select the casket or urn. If cremation, what will be the disposition of the ashes?

9. Will there be a closed or open casket at the funeral home? If covered - pall or American flag? The church may designate the procedure.

10. Select the clothing or uniform for the deceased.

11. Select floral arrangements for the church, funeral home and cemetery. The church may limit the flowers at the Altar. You may advise friends to consider donations to a charity in lieu of flowers.

12. Select the pall bearers. Or if you cannot do so, request the funeral home or the military service as appropriate to provide them.

13. Write the obituary and prepare the information for the death notice in the newspaper(s) and submit it direct or through the funeral director to the newspaper.

Other City or Service

It is possible that the burial may be in a city other than where the death occurred which of course necessitates transportation arrangements. These arrangements usually are made by a funeral director or by the military service if applicable, e.g. death in a military hospital or if on active duty. On occasion the burial and the memorial service may be held in different locations, which necessitates appropriate timing and some duplication of tasks. Memorial services may be held in more than one location if the person was prominent or well known or resided in more than one location.

Information Needed

Information to provide the funeral director regarding the deceased:

Full name

Date and place of birth

Date of death

Father's full name

Mother's full name

Names of survivors - spouse, children, grandchildren, sisters, brothers, grandparents

Memberships - Church, clubs, community and service organizations

Names of newspapers

Social security number

Military service or serial number

Chapter *Six*

NOTIFICATIONS

Categories to Notify

Some notifications must be made immediately, such as set forth in paragraphs 1 and 2 below, and others can be made as time permits, but as soon as possible. This list is not all inclusive but may suggest others that have been omitted. Notifications seem to fall into categories, for example:

1. Those notifications related to the death and to the funeral, to include the immediate family if not present, extended family, relatives, employer and employees and friends.

2. The local newspaper or papers in the community and perhaps in the original home or hometown or location of a second home, usually through the funeral director.

3. Life insurance companies which insured the life of the deceased. Notification is still needed if the policy is a "second to die." There may also be policies that cover travel and accident. See sample letters (initial letter and claim letter) in Appendix.

4. Banks and credit card companies. Note that some banks, AAA, and credit card companies provide modest amounts of insurance, or flight insurance. See sample letters to financial institutions and credit companies in Appendix.

5. Stock brokerage accounts. Call account executive or financial adviser.

6. Benefit claims. Benefits may be offered by employer or military service. Contact the agency for information and necessary forms. See Chapter 14.

7. Organizations and clubs in which the deceased held memberships, subscriptions and licensing agencies where applicable. See letter in Appendix.

Friends and Family

There are many different situations which may exist, varying with lengthy illness - or with sudden death, with family living in the community or in other areas of the world. Prior to or at the time of death, depending on the circumstance, immediate family, friends, relatives and close friends require a call providing information as to the situation, and to advise them of the death, or once funeral plans are completed, of the time and place. Honorary pallbearers if asked to serve must be provided with information.

Who in the family is to be notified and **how** should be governed by the immediate family. They might ask a close friend or friends to make the calls or choose to call personally, depending on how they feel. These calls are difficult and painful to make and there often are special considerations concerning the recipient, such as age, physical condition, emotional makeup, recent problems and living arrangement. If a person is living alone, elderly or ill, it may be appropriate to call someone who can advise them in person.

Clergy and Funeral Home

Notify the clergy and the funeral home selected as soon as possible. They can assist, provide guidance and help to plan religious and burial services, as discussed in the previous chapter.

Newspaper

The death notice will be prepared by the funeral director and submitted to the desired newspaper or papers if the information is provided. The newspaper will charge for the death notice based on the number of lines. The director can arrange billing to the funeral home and request reimbursement by the estate.

The obituary, an article concerning the deceased, may be published if the deceased had importance in the community or was newsworthy. The information can be compiled, or a draft written, and submitted to the newspaper through the funeral director. There is no charge for the obituary if it is published. Review it before publication.

Call the funeral home or local newspaper staff for information concerning their policy and charges for the death notice.

Insurance Companies (See Chapter 13 and Appendix)

In notifying insurance companies it is necessary to have the *policy number*. The policy usually is required at some point, although one insurance company advised that they have paid claims on lost policies and some do not require the policy to be surrendered. If you advise the agent who services the policy or the agency, they will advise you regarding the claim, or you may contact the servicing office, or the home office of the company.

A copy of the *Death Certificate* should be attached to a letter addressed to the insurance company advising of the death of the policy holder and including the policy number and date of death. Request instructions and forms required to complete a claim, and ask for confirmation of the principal value of the policy, accrued interest or dividends, and outstanding loans. Send the letter by certified mail. The information will be submitted to tax authorities as confirmation of the value of the policy. The company will inform you regarding surrender of the policy and payment of claim.

A follow up letter attaching the completed forms and other information required by the company is used to submit the claim. Also request IRS Form 712 for each policy to be submitted with the U.S. Estate Tax Return, Form 706. (See letters in Appendix).

Life insurance policies may specify how the proceeds are to be paid to the beneficiary or they may offer an option or options to the beneficiary.

If proceeds are payable to the estate, a lump sum payment may be requested and proceeds deposited in the estate bank account. If proceeds are payable to a Trust they would be deposited to the Trust account.

Stock Brokerage Accounts

Securities may be held in an account with a brokerage firm in the name of an individual, as a joint account, as a trust account, or in a business or corporate account. Notification to the brokerage firm would include the account name and number, a copy of the death certificate and letters testamentary. Prior notification can be made by telephone to the account executive or broker handling the account. What is to be done with the account will be based upon the ownership and will be discussed under Collection of Assets, Chapter 9.

Banks and Credit Card Companies

Some Banks, credit card companies and AAA offer policies with small amounts of insurance to depositors, card holders or members. Be sure to check on these and travel and accident policies if applicable. Some outstanding loans are insured, so ascertain whether they are.   In administering one estate I was pleased to learn that a substantial bank loan had been insured and was automatically paid off by insurance. Advise the banks and savings accounts to change the title of the account to the survivor if it was a joint account with right of survivorship, or to close the account and forward a check for the balance in the account and accrued interest. Request confirmation by letter of these amounts, principal and interest as of date of death.

Notify credit card companies by letter sent certified mail and surrender the credit card. Cards may be cut in half or otherwise mutilated to prevent use. Ask for confirmation of outstanding debt. If the spouse wishes to continue the use of the account, submit the request asking to change the account and issue a new card. Some companies including retail stores have their own charge cards and would be treated in similar fashion. (See sample letter in Appendix.)

If you're not aware of which credit cards were held, consider American Express, Visa, Master Card, Diners, Bank Cards, oil companies, telephone companies and department stores. Credit cards may be found in wallets, purses, brief cases, desk drawers, bureau drawers, jewelry boxes or auto glove compartments.

Benefit Claims

Benefits available often are not paid automatically and must be requested in writing, usually using a particular form. Some investigation may be required to determine the benefits available. The employee may have company benefits to include accrued pay, bonus, sick leave or annual leave, health benefits if there was prior illness and insurance benefits. Contact the employer or employer's personnel office to determine what is payable and the requirements for payment. Active duty military personnel, reserves and veterans may be eligible for benefits based on service. Contact the finance office or casualty office at the nearest military installation or appropriate 800 number. See Chapter 14, Filing for Benefits.

Memberships, Organizations and Clubs, and Subscriptions

A letter to organizations and clubs requesting cancellation of membership should include the membership number, address and type of membership and date of death. Enclose the membership card and request confirmation of any outstanding indebtedness. (See letter in Appendix). Some clubs may have a bond or benefit payable.

Memberships may include business clubs, social clubs, country clubs, town clubs, fraternal orders, women's organizations, national service organizations such as Rotary, Kiwanis, or Lions and athletic clubs.

Notify the licensing agencies regarding any professional or service license held and return the licenses by certified mail for cancellation.

Notify charities in which the deceased was involved. Some may hold an insurance policy payable to the charity.

Write the circulation manager of each magazine or periodical and enclose the corresponding address label to request change of name or cancellation of subscription.

Chapter *Seven*

OBTAINING DOCUMENTATION

The Paper Trail

Despite the computer, the paper trail continues and documentation is a part of life. Documents are also needed in death. Previously mentioned were the a*dvance directive*, or *living will*, the *last will and testament*, and t*rust* a*greements*. There are other documents which exist and must be located and some to be obtained. Certain actions will require certified copies of documents; these include transfers of ownership, filing claims and obtaining benefits. Required documents include the following:

Will

The most important document that you will need is the *will*, or *last will and testament*. It is very helpful if the decedent had a properly prepared and executed will and an original is in your hands or on file at the office of the decedent's attorney or in the custody of the spouse or a relative. If the will is in a safe deposit box registered in the name of the decedent there may be a delay in getting access. In some jurisdictions boxes are sealed and arrangements must be made with the appropriate official for access to and inventory of the box prior to release of the box and contents.

If the location of the will is not known to the executor, it is necessary to search. Check with the deceased's attorney, personal files, home office, office where employed or safe deposit box either prior to death if you have access or when the box is inventoried.

If the will can not be located or none is validated then the appropriate court will appoint an administrator and distribute the estate in accordance with the laws of the state.

The will provides direction to the executor regarding payment of debts and funeral expenses, specific bequests, and the division and distribution of the estate. The will also may provide specific powers to the executors or trustees, direct the establishment of a trust or trusts, and cover the payment of fees or compensation to fiduciaries and trustees. The will is the document which provides the basis of authority for the executor to act after it has been accepted for probate and *letters testamentary* or *letters of administration* are issued by the court appointing the executor.

Trust

A *revocable trust*, also referred to as an *inter vivos* or *living trust* or *grantor trust* , may have been established by the decedent. This type of trust is commonly used for control of assets and for reduction of estate taxes upon the death of the second spouse, as the assets of the first do not become a part of the estate of the second spouse to die. Assets in the trust do not have to be listed and are not included for probate but are included in the gross estate for computation of estate and inheritance taxes. Upon the death of the grantor, a revocable trust becomes irrevocable and the provisions cannot be changed. Assets can be added, however, by a "pour over" clause in the will, which specifies that certain assets are to be added to the trust. The executor should note the provisions of the will and determine whether it provides for such distribution. If you as executor also were named as trustee of the trust, administration of the trust becomes your continued responsibility.

Death Certificate

The Certificate of Death is issued by local authority stating the cause and the date of death. The funeral director is required to obtain a death certificate and will obtain copies for you (request 10 to 25). There is a cost for each certificate. You are likely to need certified copies for a number of purposes and later may have to obtain additional copies through your attorney, the local registrar or the issuing agency such as the Bureau of Vital Statistics. A certified copy of the death certificate will be required by insurance companies and agencies providing benefits, and for closing or transferring financial accounts or securities.

Letters Testamentary

The will of the decedent nominated you as the executor. The *letters testamentary* legally appoint you as executor and indicate that you have been duly qualified according to law. They are issued by the "Register for the Probate of Wills and granting Letters Testamentary and of Administration in and for the County" - or equivalent office. The will is filed with the proper office, Probate Court, Orphans Court, County Clerk or Register of Wills. Witnesses may be called to verify their signatures and that of the testator unless the will is self proving.

Letters testamentary are required for almost every action relating to assets, insurance or benefits, so you will require multiple copies. Generally each activity requires a copy which is certified and dated within 60 days of the current date. Therefore it is wise not to stockpile too many because they are relatively expensive and perishable. It is necessary to continue to request them as required.

In one estate in which I was involved , there were stock certificates issued by almost 80 different companies in the safe deposit box. A separate *letter (letters testamentary)* was required for each stock certificate. In several instances there were delays in the transfer of the stock ownership to the estate account. The letter would expire after 60 days and another had to be obtained. Additionally, a certified death certificate, stock transfer form, and an affidavit of domicile were required for each transfer.

Power of Attorney

A power of attorney often is used to enable one person legally to handle the affairs of another; it may provide specific or general powers. A *durable power of attorney* permits the *attorney-in-fact* to act when the grantor, or person granting the power, is disabled, deemed incompetent or in a coma. A power of attorney expires upon death of the grantor.

Other Important Documents

Deeds for Real Estate and Title Policies

Proprietary Lease for Co-op Apartments

Tax Information and Tax Returns for Previous Year and Current Year

Marriage Certificate

Divorce Decrees

Birth Certificates of Beneficiaries

Certificate of Service if Military veteran, DD 214, Retirement orders

Insurance Policies - Medical, Life and Casualty; Business policies

Automobile Titles

Business related documents, e.g. Buy-Sell Agreement, Key Employee, Stock Redemption. Check the personal computer (PC) for information and inventories or other information.

Appraisals and Inventories

Chapter *Eight*

PROBATE

Definition

Probate is the process or action of the probate court which legally establishes the validity of a will. The court has the right to validate wills, and to administer the estate. The word *probate* according to the American Heritage Dictionary is derived from the Latin *probatum*, something proved and *probare*, to examine, demonstrate as good. The will is not in itself adequate authority for the executor or heirs to retitle property or to release property for distribution. The will must be validated and the executor appointed by the court through probate. Probate does not happen automatically.

Application

Application must be made to the court that has jurisdiction, which may vary according to the community where the decedent was domiciled. Usually it is the county court or probate court, the orphans court, or register of wills. The attorney representing the estate, being familiar with the process, normally files the "Application for Probate of Will Produced in Court and for Issuance of Letters Testamentary." (See Appendix). The original of the will and death certificate are submitted with the application. The application for probate would include the name and address of the decedent, brief description of property owned and probable value, and other information that may be required. The court charges a filing fee and a probate fee based upon the value of the assets.

If there are assets in another state, ancillary probate may be required.

Notice Required

The court in most jurisdictions, after the application or petition has been filed, will require a notice of the death to be filed in the clerk's office and to be published in a local newspaper and in a law journal for a specified period of time, perhaps three weeks. The purpose is to notify the public of the death, to request that creditors present information to the court concerning any unpaid debts , and to invite anyone who may consider that he or she has a claim to a part of the estate to present the claim. If there is a claim or contest of the will, the court will hold a hearing or hearings. If there is no contest or claim or unusual circumstance the court will validate the will and appoint the executor.

Validating a Will

The court ascertains that the will meets the legal requirements of the state, that it was properly witnessed and that it is the correct will, if there is more than one. The court may require the witnesses to the signing of the will to appear in court to verify their signature and witness. If the will is validated it is "admitted to probate." If there are no problems and no contest of the will, the *letters* will be issued within a reasonable period of time.

If the will is considered to be invalid, the court may determine that the decedent died "intestate," that is without a will, and the laws of the state regarding the distribution of the estate will apply. If there is no will the court appoints an administrator who has the same responsibilities as an executor.

Letters Testamentary

When the will is admitted to probate, the court will formally appoint the executor and grant *letters testamentary* providing authority for the executor to act as such under the supervision of the court. If the executor was named as "independent executor" the court may not exert active supervision, but court actions and the extent of supervision may vary with conditions and location. In my experience probate was not a problem and there was no interference with my activities by any of the courts.

Inventory Required

The court will require an inventory of assets and an assessment of their value. Typically the court sends a representative to inventory the safe deposit box contents with the executor and/or the attorney for the estate. The court may require a formal appraisal for real estate, antiques, automobiles and other items of value made by an appraiser approved by the court. Even if an appraisal is not required, in my opinion it is desirable to establish a value of the assets for estate and inheritance tax returns and to satisfy the heirs in respect to value in the sale and distribution of property. Appraisals substantiate value and provide protection for the executor.

Assets in a Trust

Assets which are in a trust that was established during the lifetime of the decedent, who was the grantor of a revocable trust (a living trust, inter vivos trust or grantor trust) are not submitted for probate. The trust upon the death of the decedent becomes irrevocable and the designated trustee or trustees assume active management in place of the grantor. The provisions of the trust document then govern the administration of the trust. These assets are not subject to probate (but are subject to estate and inheritance taxes if applicable).

The executor should not become involved with any trusts set up by the decedent as irrevocable trusts as the assets are not a part of the estate.

Executor and Attorney Fees

The state may have a guideline for, or a limit on, the fees paid to the executor and to the attorney. Fees are typically a percentage of the gross value or of the net value of the estate. Attorneys usually are cognizant of the prevailing fees and can provide guidance to the executor. The court may establish the maximum fees permissible and reduce the fees claimed if they are not within the guidelines.

Chapter *Nine*

COLLECTION, VALUATION, SAFEGUARDING OF ASSETS

Fiduciary Responsibility

An executor is in a fiduciary position: a *fiduciary* is one holding a special position of confidence, trust and responsibility. The executor's duty is to settle the estate of the decedent and to make distributions in accordance with the terms of the will and until that has been accomplished to preserve the assets of the estate. These assets may include an operating business, commercial or residential real estate, automobiles, boats, planes, antiques, art, objects of art, jewelry, furnishings and personal effects.

Collection of Assets

The executor's duty is to collect or assemble the assets, to take immediate control of the assets and to adequately protect them until the appropriate disposition has been made. The asset inventory will include the contents of safe deposit boxes and personal property. In order to locate assets, review financial data, financial statements, incoming mail, checkbooks, deposits and cancelled checks, income tax records and tax returns and personal and business files for clues. If you are the spouse of the decedent you may have knowledge of the assets in the estate, but then again you may not. If the decedent had a penchant for confidentiality in personal affairs you may have a treasure hunt ahead.

Valuation

A valuation of the assets is made at the date of death and may also be made at an IRS approved alternate date - which at this time is six months after the date of death. The executor can choose which date to use; of the two alternatives, one ordinarily would use the lower value for payment of taxes. This choice of an alternate date may be especially useful in the case of stocks and real estate in a changing or volatile market.

Transfer of Assets

Transfer assets other than real estate and personal effects, such as cash, accounts collected, bank and savings accounts, and securities, in to the name of the estate, and close in to a trust, if so specified. A certified copy of the letters testamentary, tax waivers, affidavit of domicile, death certificates or other documents may be required to accomplish transfers. Assets require an appraisal or valuation to establish values for the probate court and for Federal Estate and State Inheritance Tax. The taxing authorities of the State and the Internal Revenue Service (IRS) need a valuation of the estate assets. The Probate Court will require a filing of the Inventory with valuations.

Assets or Asset Types and Appraisal Sources

The following indicates the asset types requiring appraisals or confirmation of value and possible source(s) of appraisals:

Insurance Proceeds - Life insurance is a principal asset in many estates. Contact the Insurance company or companies, and the Veteran's Administration if applicable. Complete required forms and provide requested documents, which will include death certificates and may at some point, the policy. Request Form 712, confirmation of the principal amount and dividends accrued, and the outstanding balance of any loan against the policy including accrued interest. Review options offered. The insurance company may offer a favorable rate of interest pending decision as to proceeds.

Commercial Real Estate - MAI (Member of Appraisal Institute) Appraiser.

Residential Real Estate - MAI Appraiser.

Securities - Stocks and Bonds - Brokerage house. Stocks - average of high and low prices on date of death and alternate date. Bonds - bid price.

Bank Accounts, Saving and Loan - send letter to request balance at date of death, and accrued interest to date.

CD's and Annuities - request from source.

Automobiles - request appraisal from dealer.

Antiques and Art - approved appraiser for the style and period.

Jewelry - approved appraiser.

401k, Profit Sharing and Other Retirement Benefits - request through employer.

IRA or SEPIRA - Bank or brokerage firm administering account.

Furnishings, China and Silver - appraiser or dealer depending on quality and significance.

Personal Effects - appraiser if of significant value, or dealer.

Safeguarding Assets

Until asset disposition is made in accordance with the provisions of the will, the assets must be safeguarded. Review the insurance policies which cover real estate including the residence and adjust them if necessary. It is possible that insurance coverage for a residence will no longer be in effect if a residence is unoccupied for a period of time, perhaps 30 days. Contact the company for the policy adjustment required to prevent loss of coverage. The residence may require a security system if it is to be vacant for an extended period. In some instances burglaries have occurred during the funeral service (burglars read obituaries and death notices) and you may want someone physically present in the home during the service.

Commercial property is likely to be in use. Contact the management firm if any and make necessary arrangements for safety, physical security and insurance.   If there is an operating business which the decedent managed, appoint a temporary replacement manager and supervise the operation.   If the will does not require its retention, place commercial property on the market for sale through a *commercial real estate broker*.   A *business broker* may be required to sell an operating business.   See Chapter 18, Disposition of Assets.

Chapter *Ten*

FINANCIAL ANALYSIS OF AN ESTATE

Financial Requirements

It is helpful to make an analysis of the assets and liabilities of the estate as soon as possible. Initially it may be a ballpark estimate but you need to know what you will be working with in order to make decisions and to make a rough estimate of the estate taxes due. In a typical situation there is an urgent need for money to pay expenses and to provide for the immediate family, whose expenses will be higher than usual, perhaps to pay for travel of dependent children, purchase clothes for the funeral, flowers. Regular monthly expenses such as mortgages, utilities, food, gasoline and so forth continue and require payment. Joint accounts with right of survivorship or separate accounts with adequate funds if they exist are helpful to the survivors in getting through this initial period. A trust is also helpful.

Distributions

My experience has been that it is typical for beneficiaries to start lobbying for distributions very soon after the funeral. They do not understand the reason for a delay and may have immediate requirements for cash for many creative purposes, such as a new car, house, boat or race horse. However, prior to making any distributions the executor must be assured that all debts, bequests and State and Federal taxes can be paid from the funds that will be available. It is easier to keep the peace if you are able to make some initial distributions in a reasonable period of time, but be aware that you are liable for improper distributions.

Tax Liability

More important than distributions is the tax liability. The tax liability should be estimated and an initial determination made of action required to pay the taxes; it may be necessary to sell assets. Estate taxes are due nine months after date of death and this date comes up very quickly. See Chapter 15, Payment of Federal Estate and State Inheritance Taxes, and Appendix.

Summary of Assets, Liabilities, Income and Expense

Make a list of the principal assets of the decedent and their estimated value, and the estimated Income to the estate, bequests stipulated in the will, debts of the estate and current and projected expenses. For example:

Assets and Estimated Income

Principal Assets	Value
Cash	$
Checking Accounts	
Savings Accounts	
Real Property - Cash Value	
Insurance Proceeds	
Securities Accounts	
Tangible Personal Property	
Benefits	_____
Total Assets	$

Estimated Income	Value	
Accrued Salary	$	
Interest		
Dividends		
Refunds	_____	
Total Estimated Income		$_____
Total Assets and Income		$

Bequests, Debts and Expenses

Bequests

List of bequests	$_____	
Total Bequests		$

Debts and Expenses

Funeral Expense	$	
Debts		
Probate Costs		
Property Maintenance		
Selling Expenses		
Fees - Attorney and Executor	_____	
Total Debts and Expenses	_____	
Total Bequests, Debts and Expenses		$_____
NET CASH AVAILABLE		$
Estimated Taxes - State and Federal		$_____
Net Available for Distribution		$_____

Estimate of Financial Condition

Making an estimate as outlined will provide a general idea of where you stand financially. After the valuations, appraisals and confirmations are completed, and you have sold securities and real properties as required, you can make a more complete estimate, a similar analysis which will be closer to the final summary. After each analysis has been made there are likely to be additional assessments of taxes, refunds, additional income or other income and expense that you didn't foresee. But at each stage you can make an assessment of taxes due and payable and amounts likely to be available for distribution. It is highly desirable to have the assistance of an attorney and/or a CPA who can prepare the State and Federal tax returns. The rules are complex and it is essential to be accurate. It is also helpful to have someone on your side if there are disagreements or disputes with the tax authorities.

Accounting and Filing System

From the beginning of the administration of the estate it is essential to set up and maintain an accounting system and a filing system. You may have a simple accounting system using a spread sheet or use a program on your PC. In any case, you must record the amounts received from the collection of assets and the collection of income, and you must record each disbursement or expenditure by category.

There are so many variables in the size and complexity of estates that it is difficult to generalize but there is a common responsibility.   The executor must account for the collection of assets, for the receipt of income, for each expenditure and for all distributions. A summary of the estate accounting is required for the beneficiaries and the data is necessary for filing tax returns.

A simple system might use a spread sheet for **Receipts - Collection of Assets and Income** with columns for date, source, and deposit amount and for categories of assets, such as insurance proceeds, sale of securities, settlement of real properties, sale of personal property, and bank and savings accounts. The same spread sheet could include columns for **Income** to the estate, e.g. dividends, interest and other sources. All receipts would be deposited in the estate bank account and all disbursements made from that account.

A spread sheet for **Disbursements** would include date, payee, check number, and columns for each category of expense such as administration, property maintenance, debt, taxes, etc. and columns for bequests and distributions to beneficiaries. The net of the beginning balance plus receipts, less disbursements should reconcile with the bank balance per statement each month. See Appendix for format.

A program for your PC could use similar categories and provide the data required.

Estate Summary

The Summary of the Estate would show:

Charges :

Collection of Principal Assets $

Collection of Income _____

$.

Claim Credit and Allowances:

List the Bequests, Debts and Expenses, $
 (including taxes)

Distributions to Beneficiaries _____

_____

Balance - Cash for final distribution $_____

Chapter *Eleven*

PROVIDING FOR IMMEDIATE FAMILY & BUSINESS NEEDS

Requirements of the Family

Writing on this subject is like shadow boxing. There is no target to hit. Each situation is unique; therefore these comments are understandably general in nature. In administering any estate it is necessary to assess the situation, plan a course of action and then act. Sometimes the rules have to be bent. You may not accomplish all that you set out to do in the time frame planned. The thing to remember is that you are legally obligated to carry out the wishes of the decedent as expressed in the last will and testament and according to law. You may find, however, that the deceased's planning was not great, the situation may have changed since the will was written and unforeseen things occur. So you sometimes have to bend to accommodate the living who are the beneficiaries.

Except where Dr. Kevorkian is involved, the time of death is usually unplanned and unknown. It is a shock even when expected. If a death follows a long illness, the payment of bills and other actions may have been delayed. Thus the one who is left has to pick up the pieces - perhaps with little knowledge of what has been done or needs to be done. If that person is the widow or the widower, she or he may have more knowledge than someone outside the family, but the surviving spouse is not in a frame of mind to handle immediate financial and other matters. This guide was written to be generic, and largely from the standpoint of the independent lay executor rather than that of a spouse or family member. The problems are the same but in caring for the needs of the immediate family the independent may not be cognizant of their requirements.

Assuming that you are not a family member you should interview the spouse and other beneficiaries to ascertain their needs. If the decedent had the **only** checking account with no other signatories there could be no immediate access to cash. You can determine whether there were separate accounts, joint accounts or joint accounts with right of survivorship. If cash is available you can proceed on course. If not, proceed to "Plan B."

If cash is required, after appointment of the executor assets can be pledged or sold to obtain cash. Insurance companies pay very quickly if there are no problems. The local banker might provide a loan for a short period of time. Until the appointment as executor has been made there are limitations on what the executor can do. The beneficiary may have more leverage and can use the will as evidence and pledge the inheritance to secure a loan. There are solutions which the executor may help to find.

However it happens or whatever the situation, it is possible to survive the initial period. If there is a surviving family and the principal bread winner has died, there is a need to ascertain the requirements to maintain the house and car, pay school and college tuition, buy food, gas, make installment payments and pay debts. Some source of cash is required and must be obtained. If there were no assets probably you wouldn't have been named executor. If you were named and there are no assets, file for benefits.

As is often the case, an elderly parent has died and has named one of the children as executor. Chances are the decedent lived alone and had no dependents. Notice that I said *dependents* and not *beneficiaries*. The likely problem then is to dispose of the contents of a house, probably accumulated over a period of years, and to sell the house.

Each case is different. There are obstacles, usually surmountable, and you continue on until you get to the finish line. You need to stay alert and flexible and wear your hat as a negotiator and conciliator if there is more than one beneficiary. There are many situations and ingenuity often is required.

Business Requirements

If the decedent had an operating business, there is an extended family to include employees, who also have needs. You may have to pay salaries, give notices, pay severance pay or operate the business until it is disposed of as called for. Note that the beneficiaries can hold the executor liable for inadequately insuring or protecting the property and for losses from continued operation of the business if the will does not require it. The same liability applies to retention of commercial real estate. In these matters you are wise to retain legal counsel.

Ascertain whether a buy-sell agreement exists, if there was a stock redemption plan or if there was a key employee insurance plan or other agreement.

Chapter *Twelve*

COLLECTION OF INCOME

Income to the Estate

The date of death is the important date in administering an estate. Assets are valued as of the date of death, or as of an IRS approved alternate date, which now is six months hence. Estate taxes and inheritance taxes are based upon and taxes are paid upon the value of the assets. In addition to the assets in an estate, there is likely to be income to the estate from various sources. This income must be collected and accounted for. Income to the decedent up to the date of death is included in the decedent's tax returns or in the valuation of the estate for estate and inheritance taxes if income tax returns are not filed. Income subsequent to the date of death is income to the estate and reported as such. It may be used for payment of taxes or expenses, distributed to the beneficiaries or to a trust if one has been established. The executor is responsible for the collection and the distribution of income from all sources and for the payment of income taxes, debts, expenses and bequests.

Typical Sources of Income

Salary accrued to the decedent from employment

Commissions and bonus payable

Accrued leave or sick leave paid

Retirement income accrued

Military pay - active duty or retired accrued

Social Security

Operation of a business

Rental income from investment property

Annuities

Dividends from investments

Interest from investments, banks and savings & loan associations

Trust income

Commercial real estate

Installment contracts

Contracts and residuals

Deferred income

Income tax refunds

Insurance refunds (homeowners or auto, if cancelled)

Cancellations of dues and subscriptions

Legacies

Awards

Rent Escrows

Other

Reviewing Potential Sources

It is necessary to become familiar with the activities, business operations, employment and investments of the decedent and to determine the potential sources of income. The process of collection is based upon the source. If a business were in operation and continued to operate until it was sold, the income would accrue to the business.

A place of employment ordinarily would pay income to the date of death of the decedent, if the decedent was still employed or on leave, and would pay accrued income and bonuses due. Payment of deferred income would depend upon the agreement.

Military pay for active duty or retired personnel is paid to date of death. Any routine monthly check which was not cashed must be returned and a new check issued for the appropriate period. If checks are automatically deposited in a bank, the military service would request a refund of any overpayment.

Payment of dividends and interest on investments would continue until the investment is sold, or transferred. Securities should be transferred to an estate account as soon as practicable or to the beneficiary.

Insurance companies may pay interest on the principal amount of a policy from date of death until date of payment of face amount, plus dividends accrued, less the amount of policy loans and interest payable.

Usually in order to collect accrued income or benefits it is necessary to request payment either by letter or by form, to provide proof of death and of the appointment as executor. Interest on bank accounts should be paid from the date that the last payment was due to the date that the account is closed or CD is redeemed. In the event of death, penalties for early redemption of CD's are waived by some institutions.

Some exploration may be necessary to find the sources of income and to collect it. It is difficult to discuss how to do it in the abstract as there are infinite sources. Usually the sources are apparent and you can find out what is necessary for you to do by a visit to the source or by telephone calls.

Chapter *Thirteen*

COLLECTION OF INSURANCE

Restrictions on Payment

The proceeds of an Insurance Policy on the life of a person normally are paid upon proof of death unless there are circumstances which lead to a question as to the cause of death. Some insurance policies have restrictions on payment, such as suicide within two years of issuance, piloting a private plane, or a preexisting condition which was not revealed at the time the policy was issued. Usually there should be no problem in collecting the proceeds. Claims are paid to the designated beneficiary or beneficiaries after appropriate documentation.

Submission of Claim

A claim against a policy can be originated by a telephone call to the agent, branch office or home office of the insurance company, or by letter. The company will provide advice as to their requirements which usually include a certified copy of the death certificate and letters testamentary, and completion of the necessary forms. The initial letter to the insurance company advising of the death of the insured would include the name of the insured, date of death and policy number. The letter should request advice of the principal value, accrued interest and dividends. A copy of the response can then be included with the inventory and tax return to establish valuation. At some point the company may require surrender of the policy. A second letter can include necessary documentation and forms and request information concerning payments which will be income to the estate. Request form 712 if federal estate taxes are due. See the sample letters in Appendix.

Handling of Payments

If the estate is the designated beneficiary of the policy, the executor's duty is to collect the proceeds and deposit the check in the estate account. If proceeds are payable to a beneficiary the executor would provide advice and assistance to the beneficiary as required or desired in collection. Alternative payment options should be assessed. The insurance company may pay higher interest rates than otherwise available.

Payment to a Trust

If the beneficiary is a trust, the proceeds would be deposited directly to the trust account. If a testamentary trust or trusts are required to be established, the proceeds may be deposited in the estate bank account and then paid in to the trust account or accounts when established.

Types of Insurance

In addition to the usual life insurance policies there may be life policies in connection with a bank account or AAA or travel accident policies which are to be collected. In the case of accidental death some policies pay double indemnity. Thus policies must be read carefully and discussed as necessary with an agent or attorney.

Credit Insurance

Some bank loans, installment company or credit company loans require insurance to be carried by the borrower. Proceeds from the insurance policy are used to pay off the existing balance of the loan. It should be ascertained from the loan documents whether insurance was carried.

Chapter *Fourteen*

FILING FOR BENEFITS

Availability of Benefits

Benefits are likely to be available as a result of past or present military service, from government sources or from employment. Some research and questioning is necessary to determine what benefits may be available. The right to receive certain benefits may not have been known to the decedent, or the information on benefits may not have been made known to the family or to the executor.

Inquiry may lead to the collection of benefits which can be very valuable. Contact the employer or employer's personnel office, civil service, military service, Social Security or Veteran's Administration as applicable.

Benefits from Employment

The decedent's employer may have insurance benefits, life and health, which are payable to a family member or to the estate. Accrued salary or bonus, vacation and sick leave may be payable and a retirement program, or 401K may be in existence.

Government Benefits

Social Security provides benefits such as a lump sum payment for burial if eligibility exists, aid to dependent children, and income to a widow of a Social Security recipient, or to the widow of one who was eligible to receive benefits, upon reaching the age of 60.

Civil Service provides benefits to employees and retired employees.

Military Benefits

Military benefits for active duty personnel and for retired or reserve military personnel will vary based upon military service. The procedures may vary for the different armed services. Thus the following information is representative rather than complete to give an indication of what may be available. It is appropriate to contact the nearest military installation, the casualty assistance office or equivalent and inquire as to benefits available and procedures to follow. For example, check on the following benefits:

NSLI - (National Service Life Insurance) Insurance benefits

Retired Pay - payable to date of death

Survivor Benefit Plan - SBP or Dependents Indemnity Compensation. Accrued pay and allowances - if active duty.

Burial in a national cemetery

Application for Benefits

It is generally necessary to apply for benefits using the proper forms and supplying required information.

Application for Military Benefits

NSLI - National Service Life Insurance. If the decedent had an NSLI Policy in effect benefits may be applied for by contacting:

> VA Regional Office and Insurance Center
>
> P. O. Box 8079
>
> Philadelphia, PA 19101

Retirement Pay

Retirement pay stops upon the death of the recipient and any checks not cashed must be returned to the Defense Finance and Accounting Service:

> DFAS-CL/COD: ROCD
>
> P. O. Box 99191
>
> Cleveland, OH 44199 - 1126

A casualty assistance representative at the nearest military installation will provide a form 1174, Claim for Unpaid Compensation of Deceased member of the Uniformed Services or current form if this form is superseded. The beneficiary should complete the form and return it to the casualty assistance representative. Unpaid pay and allowances are due from the first of the month through the date of death.

Survivor Benefits

The casualty assistance representative will assist with the application for an annuity under the **Survivor Benefit Plan (SBP)** if the retired member elected **SBP** coverage. There is a deduction from the serviceman's monthly pay if the SBP selection is made, and a Form indicating the beneficiary would have been filed with the military service. The beneficiary could be a spouse, former spouse or dependent children.

The Retired Serviceman's Family Protection Plan (RSFPP) stopped enrollment on September 20, 1972.

If you are unsure regarding coverage and no one has been in contact, you may write to the Survivor Benefit Division:

DFAS-DE/RB

7300 E. 1ST Ave.

Denver, CO 80279-5000

or call toll free 1 800 435 3396

Burial Benefits

Retired personnel are authorized to be interred in a national cemetery. The costs of burial and the marker are provided by the Department of Veterans Affairs (VA). When requested, active installations will provide military honors consistent with available resources, which may include pallbearers, firing party, bugler and officer or noncommissioned officer in charge. For information concerning entitlements, contact the mortuary service at the nearest military installation. Funeral arrangements must be made on the local economy by the survivors who also bear the funeral expense. For those eligible, the VA may make some reimbursement.

The VA will pay a burial and funeral expense allowance for veterans who were entitled at the time of death to receive a pension or compensation, or would have been entitled but for receipt of military retirement pay.

Contact the VA regional office or local Veterans Services Office for assistance in applying for VA benefits. The regional office toll free number is

1 800 827 1000.

Social Security Benefits

To apply for Social Security benefits contact the local office or write to:

Social Security Administration

P O Box 57

Baltimore MD 21203

Toll free telephone 1 800 772 1213

To apply for benefits you will need the decedent's social security number (SSN) and the beneficiaries' SSNs, as well as certified copies of applicable documents issued by the Bureau of Vital Statistics. Marriage license, children's birth certificate, decedent's birth certificate and a copy of the prior year's tax form W-2 may be applicable.

Monthly benefits may be paid for children under age 18 or age 19 if a full time student in a primary or secondary school; for a widow or widower between the ages of 50 and 60 who meets disability requirements; and for a widow or widower who has reached 60.

The decedent must have paid in to social security for a specified period. Average monthly wage and number of dependents will determine the monthly benefit.

A lump sum death benefit may be made if the decedent was fully or currently insured, payable to a qualified beneficiary - a spouse who was living with the decedent at the time of death or an eligible child.

Chapter *Fifteen*

PAYMENT OF TAXES

Tax Return Preparation

With regard to taxes relating to the estate, for preparation of tax returns and for tax advice, I recommend the services of a CPA or an Attorney or both as necessary. This is my effort to summarize the tax responsibilities of the executor based on my experience. The executor is responsible for the payment of federal, state and local taxes and for filing the required tax returns.

Income Taxes - For Income During Decedent's Lifetime

Federal income taxes (Federal Form 1040) and state income taxes (if applicable) are based on the taxable income events of the decedent from the beginning of the current calendar year to the date of death, and for any prior year for which taxes are unpaid.

Income Taxes - For Income to the Estate

Federal income taxes are due on income to the estate of the decedent (File Form 1041 and Form K - 1 for beneficiaries) from the date of death, or transfer into the estate name, to the closing of the estate. File tax returns based on 1099's and other source data, such as broker's confirmations of stock transactions, capital gains or losses, dividends and interest, etc. State tax returns also apply in most cases. A fiscal year may be elected rather than a calendar year.

Personal Property and Other Taxes

Certain states levy tax on personal property and tax returns must be filed if applicable.

Other tax returns associated with the decedent may be required, such as Corporate, Partnership, or Trust returns, depending upon the various activities in which the decedent had interests and the complexity of the estate.

Federal Estate and State Inheritance Taxes

Federal Estate Taxes are based on the value of the estate. Form 706 must be filed within nine (9) months from the date of death. See form in Appendix.

State Inheritance Taxes are on relatively the same basis as the federal estate tax although the taxes required vary with different states. The amount paid to the state is a partial deduction from the federal estate tax.

Summary of Tax Returns Required

To reiterate, income tax returns, both federal and state, must be filed for the decedent covering the period from the beginning of the calendar year to the date of death.

Income to the estate from the date of death or transfer into the estate name to the closing of the estate is subject to income tax. U. S. Fiduciary Income Tax Return, Form 1041, and K-1's for distributions to beneficiaries are filed, as well as a State Fiduciary Income Tax Return for each year that the estate is open, until it is closed, at which time final returns are filed. K-1's are provided to the beneficiaries, who pay tax on income distributed for the year unless the tax is paid by the estate.

The estate tax is a tax on the transfer of property at death. The estate pays the tax; however the amount remaining for distribution to beneficiaries is thereby diminished by the tax paid. The beneficiaries do not pay federal income tax on their inheritances, although some states may levy tax on the beneficiaries of an inheritance.

While the recipient of an inheritance or bequest is not taxed, such beneficiaries may be liable if the estate tax is not paid, up to the amount received.

Lifetime Gifts and Unified Tax Credit, Marital Deduction

Lifetime gifts to the extent of $10,000 per donee annual exclusion (joint gifts of up to $20,000) reduce the gross estate, thus lifetime gifts may reduce the potential tax on the estate. There is no tax of an estate under $600,000, because of a unified tax credit of $ 192,800. The unified tax credit offsets the estate tax of that amount, which is $155,800 on $500,000, and 37 per cent of the amount in excess of $500,000 (but not over $750,000).

Beginning in 1998, based upon the 1997 Tax Act, the effective unified estate and gift tax exemption will increase in a series of steps to $1,000,000 in the year 2006. For 1998 the unified credit will be the equivalent of an exemption of $625,000. There is an exclusion of up to $1,300,000 for family-owned farms and businesses which meet specific requirements to qualify.

Property passing to a spouse is free from estate or gift tax because of an unlimited marital deduction (surviving spouse who is a U. S. citizen). Charitable bequests are deductible by the estate.

Determining Taxable Estate

The first step is to determine the amount of the taxable estate which includes cash, bank and savings accounts, real estate, securities, mortgages, trust accounts, art works, collections, personal effects and other assets including business investments. Life insurance is included if it is payable to the estate or if the decedent retained the "incidents of ownership" such as the right to change beneficiaries or to assign or to surrender the policy. If property is jointly owned with a spouse, the estate includes one half of the value. After taking an inventory, assign a fair market value to each asset. Previously you should have filed an inventory with the court and obtained appraisals of assets as necessary which can be entered on the tax inventory.

Estimating Federal Estate Tax

To estimate the Federal Estate tax you may use the following guide:

Total Gross Estate - total assets at fair market value

Less Total Allowable Deductions - to include executor and attorney fees, administration expenses, debts, funeral expenses, marital and charitable deductions

Equal: Taxable Estate (Gross Estate less allowable deductions)

Add: Adjustable Taxable Gifts to get tentative taxable amount

Subtract: Unified Tax Credit, Credit for State Death Taxes and Other Credits

Determine Net Taxable Estate and Net Estate Tax based on tax schedule.

Filing Federal Estate Tax and State Inheritance Tax Forms

When filing the Federal Form 706, United States Estate (and Generation-Skipping Transfer) Tax Return, include evidence of payment of the State Inheritance tax and schedules of assets included in the gross estate, and of deductions, bequests, charitable gifts and bequests and other items. Include appraisals, valuations, letters of confirmation from banks and savings and loans and life insurance statement. These returns are due nine (9) months after date of death. Check the filing date for the State Inheritance Tax Return which may be sooner.

In the cover letter to the IRS submitting the estate tax return it is desirable to request that a closing letter be issued as soon as possible and a release of the executor from personal liability in accordance with the provisions of the Internal Revenue Code, using Form 4810. The letter and release should be issued within eighteen months of filing the request.

Summary

A very brief discussion of the tax aspects relating to an estate is presented here. Compilation of the data and preparation of the returns requires a certain knowledge of the tax codes and current changes and it is wise to defer to the professional. My purpose is to present a summary of the requirements and responsibilities under federal law. State requirements will vary too widely to be covered and local codes must be followed; guidance is required from your Attorney or CPA, IRS, or local tax authorities. See sample tax forms in Appendix.

Chapter *Sixteen*

PAYMENT OF DEBTS - ADVERTISING

Validity of Debts

The typical Will directs the payment of debts, expenses of the last illness and funeral expenses from the estate of the decedent, although there is a school of thought that payment of debts should not be specified in the will. The reason given is that if not so specified there would be no legal requirement for payment of certain debts. Certainly the legitimacy of debts ought to be questioned and verification requested if necessary documentation is not available. In fulfilling my duties as executor of an estate I called to question a substantial bill for furnishings ordered for an apartment which was not the residence of the decedent. The store manager said that the furnishings had been purchased by Mr. "Blank" while accompanied by a young lady, shortly before his death. I suggested that since he now had no use for the furniture that they merely cancel the order. I expressed my regret for any inconvenience to the store and to the young lady. I expected to receive further comment but I never did, thus saving the estate over $10,000.

Liabilities

Depending upon the filing system that was in use, it may be simple or difficult to determine what the liabilities are. A review of personal papers and incoming mail and discussions with family members should reveal what is payable. There might be an accounts payable folder. The advertising notice, a legally required advertisement in a local newspaper and in a legal journal, may bring in other obligations or requests for payment. It is very important to review income tax returns and to have a discussion with the accountant, if one was involved, to find out whether there is a tax liability for a previous year or unpaid estimated tax. A tax return for the current year, for income from the beginning of the year to the date of death, is required, and for any previous year not filed. Typical indebtedness may include:

Accounts Payable to Vendors

Credit Card Balances

Utilities

Mortgage or Trust Payments Due

Loan Interest and Principal Payments

Auto Lease Payments

Margin Balances

Balances Due on Investment Purchases

Income Taxes Payable

Other

Advertising Requirements

Local jurisdictions will require notice in the probate court of the issuance of letters testamentary and advertisement in a local newspaper and a legal journal for a specific period of time, perhaps three consecutive weeks. The purpose is to advise persons indebted to the estate to make payment and to advise creditors or those having a claim of the death and to indicate where to present their claim. Normally the attorney for the estate or the executor are designated.

Funeral Expenses

Funeral expenses will depend upon the agreement signed with the funeral home and memorial park or crematorium and columbarium. Determine whether the funeral was planned in advance and if so what payments were made. Typical funeral expenses may include:

Services of Funeral Director and Staff

Use of Facilities

Casket and Vault

Motor Equipment - Hearse, Limousines, Flower Car

Cemetery Charges and Cemetery Plot

Flowers

Payment to Clergy

If death occurred in other than the home location or if the burial is elsewhere there would be additional expense for services and transportation.

Chapter *Seventeen*

PAYMENT OF BEQUESTS

What Is a Bequest?

A **bequest** is a gift made by will of personal property. The bequest may be a specific piece of property or cash. It might be a share of the estate, such as "one half of my net estate", or "the residual estate to my cousin Samantha." The will might direct the sale of certain property with the proceeds to be paid to designated beneficiaries. When the property given is real estate, it is called a **devise**.

When to Pay Bequests

Bequests other than cash may be made by the executor at any time practicable. Bequests of cash should be made only after the executor is assured that sufficient cash is available or will be available to pay debts, expenses and taxes. If cash is not a problem bequests can be made after the will has been validated and *letters testamentary have been issued.* Usually as soon as the word of a bequest gets out there is pressure from the prospective recipients for payment. The money is needed for a variety of very important reasons, often related to the purchase of an asset. The purchase seems to assuage the anguish of bereavement. Of course this is a tongue in cheek reference. Bequests may be made to church and charities. A bequest can be paid in part initially if it is necessary and it is helpful in keeping the peace to make distributions or partial distributions as soon as possible.

Bequests of Money

A bequest of money is made by a check drawn on the estate account, payable to the person designated to receive it. A cover letter should accompany the check and copies of the letter should be retained, a copy to be filed with the tax returns and one kept on file. The cancelled check can serve as a receipt for the payment of a cash bequest. See sample letter in Appendix.

Bequest of Personal Property

A **Release and Receipt** should be obtained from each recipient of personal property other than cash, and it should be retained in the estate file. A **Receipt, Release and Refunding Bond** should be obtained from each recipient of cash and also retained in the estate file. See forms in Appendix.

Chapter *Eighteen*

DISPOSITION OF ASSETS

Requirement for Sale of Assets

The sale of certain assets may be directed by the will and they must be sold and the proceeds distributed as directed in the will. The sale of assets may be required in order to pay estate and inheritance taxes. Sale of assets in an estate is required in performing fiduciary duties as executor in order to convert the assets to cash and to effect the distributions as specified by the will.

Property not specifically designated as a bequest or devise is not held by the estate, but is sold and proceeds deposited to the estate account. The executor can be legally liable for losses incurred by holding assets which should have been sold at the appropriate time or converted to cash.

Sale of Automobile

The sale of an automobile or motor vehicle owned by the decedent can be made through a dealer or directly by the executor. The transfer of title can be handled by the auto dealer, by the local AAA office or by a department of motor vehicles. Documents required include the title to the vehicle, the registration, and a certified copy of the letters testamentary and probably a death certificate.

If the vehicle was leased, the disposition would be governed by the lease, which could permit assignment of the lease, or require payment and surrender of the vehicle.

Residential Property

Who should sell the property?

The sale of residential property normally is made through a licensed real estate broker, or a Realtor, a member of the local real estate association. As the executor of an estate you have the authority to sell the property without a real estate license and if you have the knowledge and experience to handle the transaction you may want to do so. Sale by a professional, a Realtor, is often preferable, and in a difficult market a Realtor is most likely to effect a sale and obtain the market price. Discuss the prospective sale with several Realtors and get their proposals and valuations. It is desirable to have an MAI (Member Appraisal Institute) appraisal prior to these discussions, or prior to offering for sale.

If you as executor offer the property for sale, have an attorney prepare the contract and handle the settlement. If the sale is made by a broker have an attorney represent the estate to review the offers presented and to be present for settlement.

If the property passes to the heirs, either by will or by state law, it is necessary for the heirs to join in the deed.

Sale by Executor

As the executor offering a property, you have an advantage in that some prospective purchasers believe they are likely to get a better price when the property is being sold by an estate. Advertise it in the newspapers as an estate sale and place a sign on the property **Estate Sale, Shown by Appointment, telephone number _____**. You can arrange an open house to show the property to prospective buyers. Before offering the property for sale, prepare a floor plan with dimensions as a handout. Also have a flyer prepared listing the attributes and features of the property.

Preparation for Sale

In preparing a residential property for sale it is desirable to provide curb appeal. The grounds should look their best in accordance with the time of year; mowing the lawn, trimming shrubbery and hedges, and in the fall, keeping leaves cleared is important. Replacing overgrown shrubbery or shrubbery not in the best condition is helpful. The curb, sidewalks and driveway should be swept. The house, trim and shutters should be painted if necessary.

The interior of the house should be cleared of excess furniture and of clutter. Fill any wall cracks and paint as necessary. Replace carpets which are worn with new carpets of neutral color. Empty closets of excess. Wash windows. Polish floors. Use a few flowering plants. Do what is appropriate to present the property in its best light.

Sale of Commercial Property

Commercial real estate should be appraised by an MAI appraiser and offered for sale by a broker who specializes in commercial and investment property.

An operating business should be offered for sale by a business broker.

Other Types of Property

Antiques and art can be offered for sale through a dealer or at auction. It is prudent to have an appraisal and then talk to several people who are in the business. Much depends upon the location and facilities available and upon the value of the items.

Household furnishings can be offered to dealers who specialize in buying estates or through a local furniture store dealing in used furniture. If auctions are held in the area they are a possibility. Also garage sales, or estate sales, are a good way to go.

Some property, such as clothing, will not sell and it can be donated to local charitable organizations.

Chapter *Nineteen*

ESTABLISHING TRUSTS

Living Trusts

A legal title to property held by one party (the trustee) for the benefit of another (the beneficiary) is a Trust (American Heritage Dictionary). The *trust* is a legal device which provides a means for the transfer of title to property and a level of control of the assets. There are different types of trusts which can accomplish different purposes. The <u>*revocable living trust,*</u> also called an <u>*inter vivos trust*</u> was referred to in a previous chapter as a means for transferring property out of an estate, which property then does not go through probate. The *grantor* establishes a *revocable living trust*, by means of a trust document, transfers property to the trust, and as trustee continues to control and to manage the assets in the trust as long as he, the grantor, chooses or until his, the grantor's, death. The grantor while living may change or dissolve a revocable trust at any time. Upon the death of the grantor, the revocable trust becomes irrevocable and those properties in the trust then come under the control of the successor trustee. The advantages to the grantor of this type of trust are to control what happens to the properties after the grantor's death and to avoid probate of those assets in the trust.

The properties in the trust are subject, however, to estate taxes if total assets after deductions exceed a value of $600,000, based upon the unified tax credit in effect in 1997. Starting in 1998 the effective unified estate and gift tax exemption increases annually in increments to $1,000,000 in 2006, based on the 1997 Tax Act. A spouse who is a U.S. citizen can receive any amount without it's being subject to payment of tax. In the case of a married couple, properties in the trust are not included in the estate of the second to die, resulting in substantial savings in estate taxes, if the surviving spouse had only a life estate or if the trust included a "qualified terminable interest property" known as a "Q-tip" trust.

Assets in Living Trust Not Subject to Probate

As executor you would not include for probate those assets which were in a living trust as described above and would not be involved in administering the assets unless you were also named as trustee. If you were nominated as executor you may also have been designated as the alternate or successor trustee. The trustee is responsible for the management of the assets in the trust, and for their ultimate distribution, governed by the trust provisions and by the law.

Testamentary Trusts

Perhaps as executor you will find that the will calls for a testamentary trust or trusts to be established. A *testamentary trust* is one which is established by will by the *testator* (the person who made the legally valid will prior to death). The testamentary trust serves to control the assets of the decedent according to his wishes after his death. To give an example, the decedent might want to provide income only for the spouse, with the principal going to the children upon the death of the spouse. In another situation a testamentary trust could provide for income only to the children of the testator, and upon the deaths of the children, distribution of the principal to the grandchildren. This type of testamentary trust is known as a generation skipping trust. There is a tax advantage at the time the distribution is made to the grandchildren. Under current law, one million dollars can be passed without imposition of the generation skipping tax rate. Testamentary trusts do not remove assets from probate or provide tax savings upon the death of the testator; however, they could provide tax savings through a credit by-pass trust or a "Q-tip" trust.

Establishing the Trusts

At an appropriate time, most likely after bequests are made, debts are paid and the estate and inheritance taxes have been paid, the executor will establish the trust or trusts as set forth in the will. Provisions for setting up the trusts may vary and may offer an option to the executor. In one estate which I administered, for example, the will called for three trusts to be established. One trust, Trust A, was to provide a specific monthly income for life to the widow, with the principal of the trust upon her death to go to her son. As executor and trustee I had the option (specified in the will) to purchase an annuity which would provide the designated income, instead of setting up the trust. Although the annuity would have discharged my responsibility, and the trust was a continuing responsibility, I elected to set up the trust so that the son would get the principal upon his mother's death (which is what occurred). Had I chosen the annuity the son would have received nothing.

The balance of the estate was to be divided equally between two testamentary trusts, Trust B and Trust C, each of which was to provide income for life to a sibling of the decedent, and upon the death of the sibling, the principal was to be distributed to the children of the respective beneficiaries.

In establishing a testamentary trust the will serves as the governing document. An additional trust document is not necessary. A trust ID or Federal Identification Number is obtained from the IRS and as set forth in the will, specific assets or the residuary estate are transferred to the trust. The title of the assets transferred is changed to the name of the trust. The trustee as a fiduciary is responsible for safeguarding the assets of the trust and for administering the trust as specified in the will and as required by law. The provisions for establishing trusts and the tax aspects in relation to estates and trusts can be quite complex, and legal advice and counsel is necessary.

For example, this from one estate in which I was involved quoted in part from the will:

"FOURTH: I give, devise and bequeath the residue of my estate, real and personal, to my trustees hereunder, to be divided, administered and distributed as follows:

A. If my wife, _____, survives me (and here I direct that for the purposes of this Article FOURTH she shall be deemed to have survived me unless it appears unmistakably that she predeceased me), and if the Federal Estate Tax falling due because of my death will be reduced by my making this gift for her benefit, all assets in or becoming a part of my residuary estate (undiminished by any estate or inheritance taxes) shall be apportioned between two separate trusts, such apportionment being by fractional share of my residuary estate, of whatever nature and wherever situate (undiminished by any estate or inheritance taxes) determined as follows:

(1) The numerator of such fraction shall be the number which, when added to all property passing to my wife otherwise than under this Article Fourth, or which has passed to her prior to my death, but which is determined to be included in my gross estate for federal estate tax purposes, and which qualifies for the marital deduction, shall be equal to fifty percent of the value of my adjusted gross estate.

(2) The denominator of such fraction shall be the aggregate value as determined for Federal Estate Tax purposes of the assets comprising my residuary estate, undiminished by any estate or inheritance taxes."

Did you get that? The will goes on to specify how the income is to be distributed, the conditions for distribution of principal, and what is to be done with the principal upon the wife's death. The will also specified conditions for Trust B, an additional testamentary trust provided by the will to receive the residual assets, pay income for life to the beneficiary and on the death of the beneficiary, the principal is to go to the children of the beneficiary.

Need for Legal Advice

There is much more in this will (and in others with which I was involved) from which I could quote, written in language difficult to understand, but I think that by now you get the picture. You should understand that there is need for legal advice in relation to trusts and tax matters, unless you are an expert in the field. Most of us are not.

Chapter *Twenty*

CLOSING THE ESTATE

Completing the Task

During the process of administering an estate, it might seem that you will never reach the point of closing, but eventually you do; it takes time and perseverance. After you have collected the assets, filed an inventory with the probate court, paid the debts and expenses, filed the required tax returns, estate and inheritance and income tax, disposed of assets as required, made the bequests specified and the distributions to the beneficiaries, and set up testamentary trusts, you are reaching the point of closing. Title to properties is changed and assets are transferred to the beneficiaries or to the trusts. The fees to the attorney and to the executor are paid. If a living trust had been established by the decedent and there is a "pour over" clause in the will, any assets specified are transferred. For example, "All the rest, residue and remainder of my estate of every kind and description, and wherever located, including any lapsed or void legacy or devise and any property over which I have the power of disposition or appointment, after satisfying the bequests hereinabove set out and after the payment or provision for the payment of all administrative expenses and all death taxes as hereinafter directed, I give, devise and bequeath to the Trustee of the Declaration of Trust, executed by me on _____."

Final Accounting

An accounting is prepared which will inform the beneficiaries of the receipt of principal and income, payment of debts, expenses, taxes and fees. A suggested format is shown in the Appendix. To summarize, all assets are listed from the inventory, and receipts subsequent to the inventory are listed. Gains and losses on sales and other dispositions are shown; disbursements of principal are itemized and distributions of principal to beneficiaries are shown. Proposed distributions to beneficiaries are indicated along with any reserve required for payment of taxes and filing the account. It is possible that additional taxes can be levied by the Federal and/or State governments. To complete this accounting it is necessary to have accurate records. The executor may prepare the accounting or it may be prepared by the attorney. If the estate is kept open and additional income is received, additional reports to beneficiaries and additional distributions will be required.

A final accounting may also be required by the probate court and a fee charged. Determine the procedure followed by the court to close the account and to release the executor from further responsibility.

Closing Letter

It is important to request and to receive a closing letter from the Internal Revenue Service, stating that all tax liabilities have been satisfied and relieving the executor of personal liability.

After filing the estate tax return the fiduciary representing a decedent's estate may request a prompt assessment of tax under Section 6501(d) of the Internal Revenue Code by filing Form 4810. Once the request is filed the IRS has eighteen month from the date of filing to assess additional taxes or begin court action to collect. Otherwise, the IRS would have three years from the filing of the estate tax return to make assessments of any additional tax determined to be due or file court action.

CASE STUDIES

Three case studies are presented. They are based on actual situations in which I was involved. Their purpose is to place in perspective some of the information that has been given, to help clarify it, and to illustrate that which has occurred and that which may occur in real life situations. While recalling these situations was disturbing for me, they are cited for their potential value to you.

Case Study One

Living in a Virginia suburb of Washington D. C., I received a call from my sister's husband in Texas on a Sunday morning in August. He said that my mother who had been hospitalized while receiving radiation treatment had suffered cardiac arrest the previous evening and had been resuscitated but the outlook was bleak. It was possible to get on a flight to San Antonio and I spent hours on the plane not knowing what the situation would be when I arrived. I took a cab directly to the hospital, where I met my sister and brother-in-law. The attending physician allowed me to spend 15 minutes with my mother in the intensive care unit. When I saw her I thought that she looked like a young girl; she was quite lucid and rational and we had a normal conversation albeit short.

The doctor was waiting for me when I came out of the ward to say that he would like me to make a decision - whether he should endeavor to resuscitate if my mother had another incident. The question was a rude shock. My response was that I would like her to live as long as there was some quality of life. He said that she probably would not have more than six months and would have to be in a nursing home, which she was adamantly opposed to. I promised to think about it and discuss the situation with my sister. A higher power made the decision. My mother died an hour later.

I gave the hospital the name of the funeral home where my mother had made arrangements, having pre-planned the funeral. The hospital personnel called the funeral home. At the hospital, we were asked whether we wanted an autopsy to be performed. We declined because the attending physician did not believe it was necessary from a medical standpoint and we thought that she had been through enough surgery.

We had to plan the date of the funeral to allow our brother time to fly to Texas from Colorado. We made arrangements for burial at Fort Sam Houston National Cemetery next to my father. The funeral home planned a "viewing" (this is optional). The family is supposed to stand in the room with the casket and greet the people who come to pay their "last respects." I tried to stay there and couldn't and my siblings decided they were not going to. There were a few comments made later but we didn't care. It was just too difficult. Who developed that concept of protocol?

My mother kept her will and pertinent papers in a file which had been known to me and which facilitated my efforts as executor. Previously I had read the will, at my mother's request, and had an attorney in Washington who specialized in estates and trusts review it. He had recommended one major change regarding the real property. The language in the will was changed to *direct* the sale of the real property, rather than leaving it to the three beneficiaries. This directive to sell gives the power to the executor to sell and eliminates certain problems. It is far more simple to sell a property and divide the proceeds than it is to obtain agreement of three parties regarding the disposition, the timing, price, and terms, and to obtain several signatures, especially when the heirs are spread around the country. Directing the sale of the property prevents the title from passing to the heirs; title remains with the estate until the property is sold.

Another change which unfortunately I suggested was to leave all personal effects to one beneficiary and let her make distribution according to my mother's wishes "as made known to her" rather than specifying distribution in a codicil to the will. Inasmuch as I was living 1800 miles away and I knew that distribution would be time consuming I elected to give up this power. One problem arose from the attorney's use of language. He specified *tangible personal property* rather than *personal effects*. The problem encountered was a difference of opinion as to what constitutes "tangible personal property." One attorney held that savings and loan accounts were included, which was not intended. The change also caused some dissension regarding the distribution as the wishes of the decedent were not followed. A codicil specifying the distribution of personal effects would have been preferable.

Regarding the administration of the estate, I contacted a local attorney for advice as to probate, the sale of the real property and other requirements. We went to the office of the Probate Counsel of Bexar County who required an application to the County Court "For Probate of Will Produced in Court and for Issuance of Letters Testamentary." It was necessary for the witnesses to the will to appear in court to validate their signatures, and for an advertisement to be placed in the court and in the newspapers. There was no problem. Court appraisers were not required. **Letters testamentary** were issued eleven days later qualifying me according to law as Independent Executor of the estate. The attorney was appointed as registered agent as I lived out of state.

We applied to the Internal Revenue Service for a Federal ID number. A local bank account was opened in the name of the estate. The existing bank and savings accounts were closed and proceeds deposited in the estate account after the disagreement was settled. An accounting system was set up. Current bills and funeral expenses were paid and an initial distribution of cash was made to the heirs.

In order to sell the house it was necessary in my opinion to do certain things beforehand. Although recently painted, the trim was peeling and I had it repainted and the yard spruced up. Some interior changes were considered appropriate such as removal of some furnishings, painting some of the rooms and touching up others, replacing a sink with a vanity, replacing carpet in the main hall and one bedroom and having the windows washed.

The house was appraised by an MAI (Member Appraisal Institute) appraiser at my request. The appraisal was not satisfactory to me, however, as I believed that the "comparables" (recent sales of other properties in the area) used by the appraiser were not in fact comparable, and that inadequate weight had been given to the location of the property and to the excellent schools which attracted people to the district. I then held an open house for real estate brokers and asked for their evaluations, which also seemed low.

I decided to advertise the house for sale as an Estate Sale by the Executor and placed an "Estate Sale" sign on the lawn. A number of people looked at the house; six couples were seriously considering purchase, and one couple made an offer which I accepted. The offer was contingent upon settlement of the buyer's house which had been sold. I agreed to take back a first trust at an interest rate 2 per cent below the market rate which was then 16 per cent. The contingency was removed. The house was sold! Result - the house was sold in five days at a price which was 32 per cent above the appraisal. Enhancing the attractiveness of the house through minor improvements and a below market rate loan were the influential factors in producing a quick sale. The mortgage was for five years interest only (it was paid off in two years).

After the sale of the house, all the furnishings and personal effects had to be packed, shipped and transported prior to closing. This was difficult but was accomplished. The executor normally would not be thus involved, but I was also a family member and heir - which as I think about it may be a typical situation.

It remained for me to close (settle) on the house, and to file the Estate and Inheritance Tax Returns. As monthly interest payments were received, I made distributions to the heirs. The interest was income to the beneficiaries and required filing Form 1041 and K-1's. A final distribution was made when the mortgage was paid off. As my last official act I prepared an accounting for the beneficiaries. For your guidance, three trips to Texas were necessary and six weeks of my time was spent there. Many additional hours were devoted to estate matters and the total elapsed time was more than two years.

Case Study Two

In this case, the executor named in the will was appointed by the court and served but died a year later and prior to his completing the task as executor. Having been named in the will as alternate executor, I was then appointed by the court. This situation, substituting late in the game, seemed more difficult to me than being executor from the beginning because I didn't know what had and had not been completed and it was necessary to make such determination prior to any action. In addition, because of the executor's illness and hospitalization prior to his demise, more than a year's time had elapsed and no bequests of money had been paid or distributions made. Meanwhile the legatees were getting weary of waiting and two had made financial commitments in anticipation of receipt of the legacy - a dangerous thing to do.

A major complication in closing the estate resulted from the refusal of a bank in Washington D. C. to release funds on deposit in the accounts of the deceased and contents of a safe deposit box until appropriate legal procedures for the District of Columbia had been followed. It was necessary to file certain documents required for probate, to file notice in the legal reporter and to place an advertisement in two newspapers. The D. C. bank's requirement was reasonable, and based on the District laws, but the original executor had not been well enough to go to Washington and he had been fighting the system. Thus I was asked to assist a couple of months before the executor died. As I said, some of the named recipients of bequests specified in the will were becoming disgruntled. I also became disgruntled. On a day when the temperature in Washington reached 105 degrees I was trudging around the city, to the Register of Wills, to various governmental offices, to the bank and to newspaper offices.

The deceased was domiciled in Pennsylvania; the will was filed for probate in Pennsylvania and the executor's appointment was made by a Pennsylvania court. The District of Columbia required ancillary probate because the deceased had assets in the District. It was necessary to file with the D. C. Superior Court, Register of Wills, an "authenticated" copy of the will and letters of administration. The statute states "This mode of authentication is commonly referred to as 'triple seal.' **Certified copies of the foregoing documents are insufficient**." Also required were the original and three copies of the District form "Notice of Appointment of Foreign Personal Representative" (I was the "Foreign" representative). It was then necessary for me to be appointed as Agent to Accept Service of Process, to pay Court costs, and to request a Preliminary Certificate. Following this I had to personally deliver a copy of the Notice of Appointment to the Washington Law Reporter and to pay a fee, and to place a notice in a Washington newspaper. This was not the end! Assets could not be removed from the District until six months after the date of publication of notice, unless after first publication of notice, the holder of the assets was provided with an Indemnity Bond equal to the value of the property. I provided the bond. Finally it was possible to close the Washington bank account and to proceed on course.

The real estate belonging to the decedent had been sold by a local real estate broker and settled. Personal property and effects were distributed as requested in writing by the decedent. Securities accounts with brokerage firms were closed and proceeds deposited in the estate account. The bequests made in the will and distributions were made and a final accounting was rendered to the Pennsylvania court and to the beneficiaries. The overall time after my involvement as substitute executor was about four months; total time was eighteen months. There were a few ruffled feathers along the way including mine, but all was resolved.

Case Study Three

In this case the decedent had been ill and hospitalized but recovered and was better than ever for several months, but then collapsed and died from a heart attack. His only living relative was named executrix, but she had no knowledge of his personal affairs and no experience in that capacity. I was asked to assist the executrix. The will had been written ten years previous to the death of the decedent and prior to the death of his wife a year earlier. He had by a codicil, written while he was in the hospital, removed a bank as co-executor but failed through oversight to remove the bank as co-trustee of a testamentary trust to be established.

The original signed will was located but there was no record found of assets. Fortunately a key to the house was available but several days were required to find keys to the safe deposit boxes and to the stairway leading to the third floor. The banks refused access to the safe deposit boxes until letters testamentary were issued and an officer of the court was available to take inventory. The attorney for the estate was also present for the inventory so four of us tried to fit in to a small booth made available by the bank for box holders while we inventoried the contents of the box.

The box contained the deed to real estate, stock certificates, bonds, bearer bonds and coupons and jewelry that had belonged to the late wife and not distributed. We sent a list of the securities to a stock brokerage firm in New York for valuation. The stock value was based upon the average of the high and the low price of each stock on the date of death. Some companies had changed names or merged which added a level of difficulty. Bond values were based on the bid price on date of death. It was necessary to peruse incoming mail to determine which institutions had savings accounts and CD's belonging to the decedent.

The decedent's system of filing was to replace each document and each incoming piece of mail in its envelope and then to file the envelopes in a bureau drawer without regard to date or subject. Thus finding essential and pertinent documents was extremely time consuming and exasperating. We found no summary of securities holdings, bank and savings accounts and other holdings. Everything had to be discovered.

The Federal and State Income Tax returns for the previous year had not been filed; however, the decedent had been working on them before he died and all the data was on the dining room table. We gave the data to the attorney to complete and file the returns. We were too much occupied with many other things to cope with tax returns. The attorney engaged to represent the estate also filed the will for probate and requested letters testamentary.

By reviewing the files and the incoming mail over a period of time we were able to learn from interest payments the names and addresses of the institutions holding CD's and savings accounts . Then we had to find the location of each institution. We were unfamiliar with the area, and there were quite a few locations. Proceeds were deposited in to the estate account that was opened with the local bank. Initially the attorney wrote each institution a letter in which we requested the balance in the account, the accrued interest to date, and other information concerning the account as a basis for the estate and inheritance tax returns. To close the accounts we went to each location. Each institution required a certified copy of the death certificate, and a certified copy of the letters testamentary. Some required a letter requesting closing or completion of a form and signature of the executrix.

All the securities were placed in an estate account opened with a major stock brokerage firm in New York. The firm required a copy of the will and other documents. For each stock certificate, a certified copy of the *death certificate* and *letters testamentary*, dated within 60 days, was required, and an *affidavit of domicile*. The firm required a signed stock transfer certificate for each stock certificate. Some state *tax waivers* were required. Opening this brokerage account greatly simplified control of the portfolio, providing automatic deposit of dividends and interest, and monthly statements of the account. The advice provided facilitated adjustment of the portfolio.

The will provided for establishment of a *trust* with income to the beneficiary for life and then distribution of the principal to the residuary beneficiaries. The executrix was also a trustee. A trustee has the responsibility to manage the trust in a prudent manner, a fiduciary responsibility; thus the selection and holding of investments in a trust portfolio may be different from that of the individual, who can speculate if he chooses.

Our relationship with the bank named as co-trustee was unsatisfactory, so we filed a petition with the court to appoint a substitute trustee. Action by the court required a hearing and subsequently a decision was made in our favor and a court order was issued. The procedure took several years; however, required additional expense and caused a great deal of agitation. During this period the establishment of the trust was held in abeyance.

Collection of the proceeds of the insurance policies required a letter to each company which included a certified copy of the death certificate and of the letters testamentary, along with the policy number and name and address of the beneficiary and recipient. Proceeds were paid to the beneficiary or to the estate as applicable. One policy had been cancelled in exchange for an annuity payable to the decedent. Pursuit of the insurance company elicited the information that there was an accrued payment which was payable to the estate, although initially the company stated that the policy had no residual value.

To summarize the activities relating to this estate, the will was filed for probate and letters testamentary were issued enabling the executrix to act. Appraisals were obtained for automobiles, real estate, personal property and personal effects. Valuations were obtained for stocks and bonds. Notice was filed in the legal journal and local newspaper. An estate bank account was opened. Savings and checking accounts were closed and the proceeds deposited in the estate account. Insurance proceeds were collected and those payable to the estate were deposited in the estate account. Initially stock certificates and bonds were held in the safe deposit box and dividends and interest were deposited in the estate account. After discussions with several financial advisers and brokerage companies, we opened an estate account with a stock brokerage company in New York, and deposited the certificates, bonds and coupon bonds with the company for transfer of ownership to the estate account. Ultimately the account was transferred to the trust after the court decision.

The Federal Estate Tax Return (Form 706) and State Inheritance tax returns were filed and taxes paid. Income tax returns for the decedent were filed for the year prior to death and for the year of death from January 1 to date of death. Following date of death Form 1041, Fiduciary Tax Return and K-1's, copy to beneficiary, were filed each year. Personal property tax returns as required by the state also were filed. Following establishment of the Trust, the account names for the stock brokerage account and bank account were changed to the trust. A final income tax return for the estate was required. Subsequent federal tax forms 1041, and state tax forms will be filed for the trust.

After ascertaining the adequacy of funds, bequests made in the will were paid to those named and distributions of personal effects and personal property were made. Distributions to the income beneficiary began and fees were paid to the attorney and the executor after the Federal Estate and State Inheritance taxes were paid. The elapsed time in administering this estate was almost eight years.

These case studies indicate how different each situation is, as well as the similarities, and the complexity of some. The commitment of time and energy was great but there was a feeling of satisfaction in fulfilling a responsibility which I had accepted, and in serving the needs of those who were gone and those who remain.

GLOSSARY

ADMINISTRATION - of an estate is the management of the affairs and settlement of the estate of a person who is deceased

ADMINISTRATOR - one who is appointed by a probate court to administer the estate of a deceased person

ANCILLARY - subordinate or auxiliary

ASSETS - property which one possesses, and claims against others

AUTOPSY - the medical examination of a dead body to determine the cause of death

BENEFICIARY - one who is designated to receive or who receives the benefits or enjoyment of property through a trust, inheritance or insurance policy

BEQUEST - property given to a person by will

CREDITOR - a person to whom a debt is owed by another person

CURTESY - a man's life interest in real property owned by his wife, whose children of the marriage at her death have right of inheritance

DEBTOR - a person who owes money or a debt to another

DEED - a document related to property sealed as a means of contract or conveyance

DOWER - the widow's life interest in real property owned by her husband

EXECUTOR - a person designated by will to administer the estate of the deceased

FIDUCIARY - one who stands in a special position of trust, responsibility and confidence; one who holds something in trust for another

GRANT - to bestow, confer, to transfer property by deed

GRANTEE - the person to whom a grant is made

GRANTOR - the person who makes a grant

GROSS ESTATE - total value of an estate before debt

HEIR - one who inherits property, either real or personal

HOLOGRAPHIC WILL - a will written in the handwriting of the maker or testator

HYPOTHECATE - to pledge a thing as security for a loan while retaining possession

INDEMNITY - insurance or other security against possible damage or loss; a legal exemption from liability for damages

INTESTATE - having made no legal will; to die without a will

JOINT TENANCY - ownership held concurrently by two or more persons

LEGACY - a gift of personal property by will

LEGATEE - the inheritor of a legacy

LETTERS TESTAMENTARY - document issued by a probate court appointing an executor and providing authority

MORTGAGE - a conditional pledge of property to secure payment of a debt or obligation

MORTGAGEE - a person who lends money on a property and receives a mortgage in exchange

MORTGAGOR - one who gives a mortgage; owner of property mortgaged

PER CAPITA - per person, equally to each heir

PERSONAL PROPERTY - personal, movable or temporary, as opposed to real property

PER STIRPES - by class, or right of representation

POSTHUMOUS - after death, occurring or continuing after death

POWER OF ATTORNEY - instrument authorizing another to act as agent or attorney

PRINCIPAL - the person who constitutes and gives authority to an agent to act for him

PROBATE - the judicial process to determine the validity of a will

REALTY - land as distinguished from personal property

REVOCABLE TRUST - capable of being revoked, a living trust or inter vivos trust

TANGIBLE - visible and appraisable, corporeal, of a material nature

TESTAMENT - a legal document expressing a person's wishes, a will

TESTAMENTARY TRUST - a trust created by will

TESTATE - having made a valid legal will prior to death

TRUST - a legal title to property held by one party, the trustee for the benefit of another, the beneficiary

TRUSTEE - a person appointed to execute a trust

WILL - a legal declaration of a person's wishes for the disposition of his property upon his death

APPENDIX SUMMARY

The Appendix includes examples of forms in use by various states and the District of Columbia, suggested letters which the executor can use in administering the estate, and state and federal tax forms.

APPENDIX 1

Petition for Probate and Grant of Letters

Chapter 8, PROBATE, describes the process of probate. The executor or attorney files a petition or application for probate in the court which has jurisdiction, requesting probate of the will and codicil(s) and grant of letters. The form illustrated in Appendix 1 is used in the County of Delaware, Commonwealth of Pennsylvania. Forms will vary.

PETITION FOR PROBATE and GRANT OF LETTERS

Estate of ....

also known as ....

....

....*Deceased*

Social Security No. ....

The petition of ....

....

No.	
TO:	JAMES F. PROUD, ESQUIRE Register of Wills for the County of Delaware in the Commonwealth of Pennsylvania

respectfully showeth that ...... is/are 18 years of age or older and the execut ...... residuary legatee and devisee named in the Last Will of the above said decedent dated the ...... day of ...... A.D. 19 ......

and codicil(s) dated ....

....

....

(state relevant circumstances, e.g. renunciation, death of executor, etc.)

Decedent was domicile at death in Delaware County, Pennsylvania, with h ...... last family or principal

residence at ....

....

(list street, number and municipality)

Decedent, then .... years of age died .... 19 ...... at .... o'clock ...... M.

at ....

Except as follows, decedent did not marry, was not divorced and did not have a child born or adopted after execution of the will offered for probate; was not the victim of a killing and was never adjudicated incompetent:

* The said decedent *was* domiciled in the Commonwealth at the time of h .... death, and the estimated value of all h .... personal property is $ ...., and the estimated value and location of h ...... real property situated in the Commonwealth is as follows:

* The said decedent *was not* domiciled in the Commonwealth at the time of h .... death, and the estimated value of h .... personal property in the Commonwealth is $ ...., the estimated value of h .... personal property in this county is $ ...., and the estimated value and location of h .. real property situated in the Commonwealth is as follows:

LOCATION	VALUE
....	....
....	....
....	....
....	....

WHEREFORE, petitioner(s) respectfully request(s) the probate of the last will and codicil(s) presented herewith and the grant of letters .... thereon.

(testamentary administration c.t.a.: administration d.b.n.c.t.a.)

....	....
....	....
....	....
....	....

of Petitioner(s)

* Strike out paragraph not applicable

OATH OF PERSONAL REPRESENTATIVE

COMMONWEALTH OF PENNSYLVANIA }

COUNTY OF DELAWARE } SS

The petitioner(s) above-named swear(s) or affirm(s) that the statements in the foregoing petition are true and correct to the best of the knowledge and belief of petitioner(s) and that as personal representative(s) of the above decedent petitioner(s) will well and truly administer the estate according to law.

Sworn to or affirmed and subscribed before me this .... day
of ....19.....

....
Deputy Register

....
....
....
....
....

No............

Estate of ....Deceased

DECREE OF PROBATE AND GRANT OF LETTERS

AND NOW, ...19.......in consideration of the petition on the reverse side hereof, satisfactory proof having been presented before me, IT IS DECREED that the instrument(s), dated ....

described therein be admitted to probate and filed of record as the last will of ....

....

and Letters ....

are hereby granted to ....

....

....

....
Deputy Register of Wills

FEES	
Probates, Letters, Etc. ....$	
Inventory ....$	
Debts & Deductions ....$	
Short Certificates ....$	
Affidavit ....$	
Renunciation ....$	
Bond ....$	
TOTAL ....$	

....
ATTORNEY (Sup. Ct. I.D. No.)

....
Address

....
Phone

Filed ....

APPENDIX 2

Application for Probate of Will

The form shown in Appendix 2 differs from that in Appendix 1 in format and content. It was used in the County Court of Bexar County, Texas, to apply for probate of will and for issuance of letters testamentary. It was completed by the attorney for the applicant.

NO. 1_____

ESTATE OF	§	IN THE COUNTY COURT
	§	OF
DECEASED	§	BEXAR COUNTY, TEXAS

APPLICATION FOR PROBATE OF WILL PRODUCED IN COURT AND FOR ISSUANCE OF LETTERS TESTAMENTARY

TO THE HONORABLE JUDGE OF SAID COURT:

FRANK W. BAUERS, applicant, furnishes the following information to the Court for the probate of the written will of

and for issuance of letters testamentary:

I.

Applicant is an individual interested in this estate, domiciled in and residing at 1600 S. Eads Street, Apt. 1211 South, Arlington, Virginia, 22202.

II.

Decedent died on _____ in San Antonio, County, Texas, at the age of years.

III.

This Court has jurisdiction and venue becuase decedent was domiciled and had a fixed place of residence in this county on the date of death.

IV.

Decedent owned real and personal property described generally as separate property of a probable value in excess of $.

V.

Decedent left a valid written will bearing her signature dated March 17, which was never revoked and is filed herewith.

VI.

No child or children were born to or adopted by decedent after the date of the will.

VII.

Decedent was never divorced.

VIII.

Decedent's will named applicant to serve without bond or

other security as independent executor, in which capacity applicant is not disqualified by law from serving or from accepting letters testamentary, and applicant is entitled to such letters.

IX.

There is no necessity for court appointed appraisers for this estate and it is requested that none be appointed.

X.

It is requested that MICHAEL D. BOWLES, Attorney at Law, be recognized by the Court as registered agent for service of this estate.

WHEREFORE, applicant prays that citation issue as required by law to all persons interested in this estate; that the will be admitted to probate; that letters testamentary be issued to applicant; and that all other orders be entered as the Court may deem proper.

Respectfully submitted,

/s/

MICHAEL D. BOWLES
Attorney for Applicant
JOHNSON & BOWLES
7303 Blanco Road
San Antonio, Texas   78216
State Bar No. 02743700

NO. _____

ESTATE OF   §   IN THE COUNTY COURT

                    ...J,   §   OF

DECEASED   §   BEXAR COUNTY, TEXAS

O A T H

I do solemnly swear that the writing which has been offered
for probate is the last will of   so far
as I know or believe, and that I will well and truly perform all
the duties of independent executor of the Estate of
;, Deceased.

_____

FRANK W. BAUERS

SUBSCRIBED AND SWORN TO BEFORE ME by FRANK W. BAUERS this
_____ day of _____, 1981, to certify which, witness
my hand and seal of office.

                              _____
                              NOTARY PUBLIC, Bexar County, TX

                              My commission expires: _____

APPENDIX 3

Advertising Notice

After the application or petition for probate is filed, the court may require a notice of the death to be filed in the clerk's office and to be published in a local newspaper and a law journal for a specified period of time. The purpose is to advise the public of the death, to request that creditors present information to the court concerning unpaid debts, and to invite claimants to present the claim to the court.

Request proof of publication from the newspaper.

ADVERTISING NOTICE

ESTATE OF _____, DECEASED, late of the Borough of _____. Letters Testamentary on the above estate have been granted to the undersigned, all persons indebted to the estate are requested to make payment, and those having claims to present same, without delay to:

Name and address of Executor

Or to his attorney:

Name and address

APPENDIX 4

Appointment of Registered Agent

If the executor does not reside within the jurisdiction of the probate court, the court may require appointment of a registered agent to accept service. Appointment may be requested by a letter as in Appendix 4, or by form if specified.

Frank W. Bauers
1600 S. Eads Street
Apt. 1211 South
Arlington, VA 22202

Presiding Judge
Probate Court
Bexar County, Texas
San Antonio, Texas 78205

Dear Sir:

It is my desire that Michael D. Bowles, Attorney at Law,
7303 Blanco Road, San Antonio, Bexar County, Texas, be appointed
as registered agent for service for all purposes in the estate
of   , deceased.

Sincerely,

Frank W. Bauers

FRANK W. BAUERS

SUBSCRIBED AND SWORN TO BEFORE ME this _____ day of

_____, 1981.

                          _____
                          NOTARY PUBLIC, Bexar County, TX

                          My commission expires: _____

APPENDIX 5

Letters Testamentary and Letters of Administration

After the will has been validated the court will issue a document stating that the executor, administrator or personal representative has been duly and legally appointed and has qualified according to law. This document provides the authority required by the appointed person to act and is issued in the form of Letters Testamentary or Letters of Administration.

The examples in Appendix 5 are of Letters used in Bexar County, Texas; Delaware County, Pennsylvania; Fairfax County, Virginia; and the District of Columbia.

This letter is a very important document and is required for almost every action related to assets, insurance or benefits. Generally, each activity requires a copy that is certified and dated within 60 days of the current date.

NO. 157,686

Estate of

Deceased.

Letters Testamentary

State of Texas
County of Bexar

I, ROBERT D. GREEN, CLERK OF THE COUNTY COURT OF BEXAR
COUNTY, TEXAS, DO HEREBY CERTIFY, THAT ON THE ___31st___
DAY OF ___AUGUST___ A.D., 19_ _ _____

_____

FRANK W. BAUERS . _____QUALIFIED ACCORDING

TO LAW AS ___INDEPENDENT EXECUTOR_____

OF THE ESTATE OF _____ _ _____

_____

DECEASED, AND THAT SAID APPOINTMENT IS STILL IN FULL FORCE
AND EFFECT.

GIVEN UNDER MY HAND AND SEAL OF OFFICE AT SAN ANTONIO,
TEXAS, THE ___31st___ DAY OF ___AUGUST___ A.D., 19___.

ROBERT D. GREEN, Clerk
County Court, Bexar County, Texas

By: _Vickie A. Diaz_ Deputy

VICKIE A. DIAZ

117-10

COMMONWEALTH OF PENNSYLVANIA　} ss:

DELAWARE COUNTY

I, JAMES F. PROUD, ESQ., Register for the Probate of Wills and granting Letters Testamentary and of Administration in and for the County of Delaware, in the Commonwealth of Pennsylvania, Do Hereby Certify that on the .....16th...day of... ....19........

....

....

....

....

....

w..AS....duly and legally appointed as ....---EXECUTRIX---..............of the estate of

................---...---....................................

---WHO DIED

....

late of Delaware County, Pennsylvania, and h.AS.. been duly qualified as such according to law, as can be verified by reference to the records in my office, and that the letters have not been revoked.

WITNESS my hand and seal of office, at Media in the County aforesaid, this .....23RD..............

day of ....JANUARY..............19..91........

....
CHIEF *Deputy Register*

FILE 23-88-

STATE OF VIRGINIA
COUNTY OF FAIRFAX } To-wit:

I, W. Franklin Gooding, Clerk of the Circuit Court of Fairfax County, Virginia, the same being a Court of Probate and

of Record and having a seal, do hereby certify that it appears of record in my office pursuant to law that

FRANK W. BAUERS, JR.   ha s   been duly appointed as EXECUT OR

under the Last Will and Testament of   and that he ha s

qualified as such by taking the oath prescribed by law, and by entering into and acknowledging a BOND in the penalty of

Four Hundred Thousand   Dollars, with justified and approved surety.

I further certify that the said appointment and qualification are still in full force and effect and have not been revoked.

IN TESTIMONY WHEREOF I have hereunto set my hand,

and affixed the seal of said Court hereto, at Fairfax, Virginia, this

day of

W. FRANKLIN GOODING, CLERK

By: _Franew D Myer_
                                    Deputy Clerk.

Superior Court of the District of Columbia

PROBATE DIVISION

LETTERS OF ADMINISTRATION

Estate No. _2896-89_

To all persons who may be interested in the Estate of

_____, *deceased:*

Administration of the Estate of the deceased has been granted on _December 22, 1989_

to _____

and the will of the deceased was admitted to probate on December 22, 1989.

The appointment is in full force and effect as of this date.

WITNESS:

DATED _December 29, 1989_

Register of Wills
Clerk of the Probate Division

APPENDIX 6

Certificate - Superior Court of D.C.

The certificate in Appendix 6 was issued by the Superior Court of the District of Columbia to certify that authenticated copies of the will and appointment of the Personal Representative of the deceased had been filed with the Probate Division. This certificate was required for ancillary probate, which was necessary because the deceased resided in another jurisdiction (Pennsylvania) but had assets in the District of Columbia. These assets could be released only by following the process required in the District.

Superior Court of the District of Columbia
PROBATE DIVISION

CERTIFICATE

FOREIGN NO. <u>121-88</u>

DISTRICT OF COLUMBIA, to wit:

I, <u>Constance G. Starks</u>, Register of Wills for the District of Columbia,

Clerk of the Probate Division, hereby certify that authenticated copies of the will and appointment

of _____ as Personal Representative of the Estate of

_____, deceased, have been filed, said appointment having

been made on <u>November 6,</u>, 19<u>87</u> by the <u>Register of Wills</u> Court in

<u>Pennsylvania</u> County, State of <u>Delaware</u>.

Witness my hand and seal of the Probate Division this <u>21st</u> day of _____

<u>June</u>, 19<u>88</u>.

_____
Register of Wills for the District of Columbia
Clerk of the Probate Division

NOT VALID WITHOUT
RAISED SEAL

THIS CERTIFICATE DOES NOT IN ITSELF CONSTITUTE
AUTHORIZATION FOR RELEASE OF ASSETS.

SATISFACTION OF THE ADDITIONAL REQUIREMENTS
UNDER D.C. CODE 20-343(a) IS PENDING.

FORM PD (25)-1267/Nov. 86   87—p6128 wd-234

APPENDIX 7

Letter of Indemnity

In order to release assets of the deceased who had resided in another jurisdiction but who had assets in the District of Columbia, it was necessary to file for ancillary probate and to provide a letter of indemnity or wait for six months following the publication of notice of death.

LETTER OF INDEMNITY

RE: ESTATE OF
                          DECEASED
_____ _____

I, the undersigned, FRANK BAUERS, whose address is

International,   ., Washington, D. C.

20007, individually and agent for   , Executor

of the Estate of   , agree to indemnify and

save harmless   National Bank of Washington, D. C., against

any and all loss, damage, costs and expenses which said bank may

hereafter suffer, incur or be put to or pay by reason of the

payment of the entire balances of Account No. 03-045-984 and

No. 08-943-097 now held in those accounts by said bank in the

name of 1   _ and I do further agree to pay and

discharge forthwith on demand of said bank each and every debt,

obligation or legitimate claim which shall be made, assigned or

apportioned against said bank by any claimant against the estate

of the said

Dated the   day of   , 1988.

_____
FRANK BAUERS

APPENDIX 8

Notice of Appointment of Foreign Personal Representative

The Superior Court of the District of Columbia, Probate Division, issued Notice of Appointment of Foreign Personal Representative and Notice to Creditors to me as agent for the service of process, as I had a residence in the District, while the executor (personal representative) was domiciled in Pennsylvania.

Superior Court of the District of Columbia

PROBATE DIVISION

FOREIGN NO._____

Notice of Appointment of Foreign Personal Representative and Notice to Creditors

_____ -- _____, whose address(es) (is/are)

_____ Delaware County, Pennsylvania, 19081

(was/were) appointed Personal Representative(s) of the estate of_____ :/A

_____, deceased, on __November 6__ , 19_87_,

by the_REGISTER OF WILLS_____Court for____DELAWARE____County,

State of___PENNSYLVANIA___.

Service of process may be made upon __FRANK BAUERS,__ ____ _____

, Washington, D.C. __, whose designation as District of Columbia

(Insert name and address)

agent has been filed with the Register of Wills, D.C.

~~The decedent owned the following District of Columbia real property:~~ (Omit last sentence if no real estate.)

_____

_____

The decedent owned District of Columbia personal property. (Omit last sentence if no personal property.)
~~Claims against the decedent may be presented to the undersigned and filed with the Register of Wills for the~~
~~District of Columbia, 500 Indiana Avenue, N.W., Washington, D.C. 20001 within six months from the date of~~
~~first publication of this notice. (Omit last sentence if no real estate.)~~

Date of first publication: X _____

July 5, 1988   alive(s)

_____

TRUE TEST COPY

_____

REGISTER OF WILLS

Name of Newspapers and/or Periodical:

Daily Washington Law Reporter

Afro-American

APPENDIX 9

Notice of New Employer ID Assigned

An estate is a tax entity and tax forms must be filed. Therefore, the executor requests the assignment of an Employer Identification Number. The attorney for the estate may have a block of numbers from the Internal Revenue Service (IRS). He can assign one and advise the IRS. The IRS will then send a confirmation Notice of New Employer Identification Number (EID) Assigned. Or you may contact the IRS direct. The EID is used on all Tax forms and correspondence.

18250614

Date of This Notice

If you inquire about
your account, please   10-21-
refer to this   Employer Identification Number
number or attach a ▶ 74-6305157
copy of this notice

FRANK W BAUERS IND EX
1600 S EADS ST NO 1211 S
ARLINGTON   VA   22202

575 B 555555155
     55555555

NOTICE OF NEW EMPLOYER IDENTIFICATION NUMBER ASSIGNED

Thank you for your application for an employer identification number. The number above has been assigned to you. We will use it to identify your business tax returns and any other related documents, even if you have no employees.

Please keep this number in your permanent records. Use the number and your name, exactly as shown above, on all Federal tax forms that require this information, and refer to the number in all tax payments and in tax-related correspondence or documents. You may wish to make a record of the number for reference in case this notice is lost or destroyed.

We appreciate your cooperation.

Form 5372 (Rev. 8-76)

APPENDIX 10

Sample Letter to Financial Institutions

This sample letter or one similar can be used to advise banks, savings and loan and credit institutions of the death, and of your appointment and to request confirmation of accounts, balances, and accrued interest. The confirmation on the letterhead of the institution can be used for verification of the value of the asset for submission to the probate court.

SAMPLE LETTER TO FINANCIAL INSTITUTIONS

LETTERHEAD

Date

Name and
address
of institution

Re: Estate of _____, Deceased
Date of Death _____
Account Number (s) _____

Dear Sirs:

This is to advise that _____ died on _____(date). I have been appointed Executor of the estate.

We request a statement on your letterhead providing the following information:

Title of account or accounts held by decedent.

Date that account was opened.

Balance of account as of date of death.

Interest accumulated from the beginning of the year to date of death.

This information is necessary for preparation of estate and inheritance tax returns.

Please search your records to determine whether the decedent had any other accounts with your institution in his, her name alone or jointly with others. Please advise also whether the decedent held a safe deposit box.

Thank you for your assistance and cooperation.

Very truly yours,

_____(signature)
(typed name)
Executor

APPENDIX 11

Sample Letter to Close Accounts

This letter is used to close bank, savings and loan, and credit institution accounts. Note that the request for the amount of interest from date of death to closing the account is to establish the amount of income to the estate. Certified copies of the death certificate and of the letters testamentary are usually required. Some institutions may require completion of a form and a personal visit.

SAMPLE LETTER TO CLOSE ACCOUNTS

LETTERHEAD

Date

Name and
address
of institution

Re: Estate of _____
Account Number _____

Dear Sirs:

As Executor I represent the estate of _____ who died on _____ (date). At the time of his death he, she had a credit balance in account number _____.

Please close this account and forward a check drawn to the Estate of _____. Please advise by letter the principal balance at date of death and interest from that date to date of closing.

Enclosed are a copy of the death certificate and a copy of the letters testamentary appointing me as Executor. Thank you for your assistance.

Very truly yours,

_____(signature)
(typed name)
Executor

APPENDIX 12

Sample Letter to Credit Card Companies

The letter to the credit card companies is to close the accounts of the decedent. If a survivor wishes to continue the account or change the name, the request may be made in lieu of closing.

LETTER TO CREDIT CARD COMPANIES

LETTERHEAD

Date

Name and
address
of institution

Re: Account Number _____
Name _____

Dear Sirs:

This is to advise that the holder of the referenced account died
_____(date). As Executor of the estate I request that the account
be closed. The credit card is enclosed (mutilated).

Very truly yours,

_____(signature)
(typed name)
Executor

Enclosure:

credit card

APPENDIX 13

Initial Letter to Insurance Companies

The initial letter to insurance companies serves to advise the company of the death and obtain the value of the policy for probate and estate and inheritance tax purposes. It also obtains the requirements for claiming benefits. Do not submit the policy with this letter.

INITIAL LETTER TO INSURANCE COMPANIES

LETTERHEAD

Date

Insurance Company Name
Attn: Claims
Address

Re: Policy Number _____
Name of Insured _____

Dear Sirs:

This is to advise you that _____ died on
_____(date).

Please send to me the requirements for submitting a claim for death benefits under your policy number _____, including any necessary forms.

We would appreciate your sending also the following information:

Principal value of policy

Accrued interest, dividends or premium refunds payable

Outstanding loans or liens against the policy if any.

Thank you for your assistance.

Very truly yours

_____(signature)
(typed name)
Executor

APPENDIX 14

Claim Letter to Insurance Companies

The claim letter to the insurance companies fulfills the requirement of the company through the letter and the enclosures as listed. The response should also establish the asset values for probate and estate and inheritance taxes and income to the estate. You may find that there are unexpected amounts to be paid such as terminal or postmortem dividends and interest from date of death. Or you may find that loans against the policy have reduced the anticipated payment. Some of the items listed may not be applicable. On the other hand, nothing ventured, nothing gained.

CLAIM LETTER TO INSURANCE COMPANIES

LETTERHEAD

Date

Name of Insurance Company
Address
                                        RE: Policy Number_____
                                        Name of Insured_____

Dear Sirs:

This is to submit a claim for benefits payable under Policy #_____ in the name of _____ who died on _____(date). The following documents are attached:

1. Certified copy of court appointment of executor.
2. Certified copy of death certificate.
3. Completed claim form (or documents required).
4. Policy Number _____ (if policy is required at this time).

Please make check payable to the estate of _____ (or specified beneficiary). Please itemize in your return letter the amounts paid and the deductions which are applicable, to include:

Face amount of policy

Dividends held

Terminal dividend

Refund of premium

Postmortem dividend

Policy loans or liens

Interest payable

Deferred premiums

Proceeds from policy

Interest from date of death

Please complete and enclose Form 712 to be filed with the U.S. Estate Tax Return.

Thank you for your assistance in completing this claim.

Very truly yours,

_____(signature)
(typed name)
Executor

APPENDIX 15

Sample Letter to Organizations

This letter is to cancel memberships and to collect any amounts due to the estate.

LETTER TO ORGANIZATIONS

LETTERHEAD

Date

Name of Organization
address

Re: Member Number _____
Name _____

Dear Sirs:

    This is to advise you that _____ who was a member of your organization died on _____(date). Please cancel the membership and refund if it is your policy, unexpired or prorated dues, payable to the estate. The membership card is enclosed.

Very truly yours,

_____(signature)
(typed name)
Executor

Enclosure:

    membership card

APPENDIX 16

Estate Information Sheet

This is a Pennsylvania Department of Revenue form to provide required information and is included for illustration. Ascertain the requirements of the Probate court and complete the forms necessary.

PA DEPARTMENT OF REVENUE
ESTATE INFORMATION SHEET

	FOR REGISTER'S OFFICE USE ONLY	
County Code	Year	File Number

DECEDENT INFORMATION: Enter data as it will appear on all documents submitted to the department.

Name (Last)	(First)	(Middle)

Decedent's Social Security Number	Date of Death	Date of Birth

TYPE FILING: Enter check (✓) mark to indicate the nature of the return to be filed with the department.

☐ Probate Return ☐ Joint Assets Only ☐ Estate Tax Only ☐ Litigation Purposes (No Other Assets)

LETTERS GRANTED: Enter check (✓) mark to indicate the nature of the proceedings at the Register of Wills Office. (Attach additional sheets if explanation is necessary.)

☐ Testamentary ☐ Administration ☐ No Letters ☐ Other (Please Explain)

ATTORNEY/CORRESPONDENT INFORMATION: Enter all data concerning the attorney or other individual to receive all tax information and correspondence.

Name (Last)	(First)	(Middle)	Supreme Court I.D. #

Street Address

City	State	Zip Code	Telephone Number

PERSONAL REPRESENTATIVE INFORMATION: Enter all data concerning the personal representative(s) of the estate authorized by the Register of Wills

Executor/Administrator

Name (Last)	(First)	(Middle)	Social Security Number

Street Address

City	State	Zip Code	Telephone Number

Co-Executor/Administrator

Name (Last)	(First)	(Middle)	Social Security Number

Street Address

City	State	Zip Code	Telephone Number

Co-Executor/Administrator

Name (Last)	(First)	(Middle)	Social Security Number

Street Address

City	State	Zip Code	Telephone Number

Prepared By	Date

APPENDIX 17

Affidavit of Personal Property Subject to County Tax

The affidavit is filed after inventory and appraisal of personal property, which includes jewelry, automobiles, securities and other property, other than real property. The form must be notarized and filed with the office of the register of wills.

In the matter of the ESTATE OF

. . . .

Legal Residence of Decedent . . . .

Date of Death . . . .

Affidavit of Personal Property Subject to County Tax

(To be Filed in Duplicate in the Office of Register of Wills)

COUNTY OF DELAWARE, ss:

. . . . .executor

administrator , of the estate of the above-named decedent, being duly sworn according to law depose and say that included in the inventory and appraisal filed in the above estate or in the affidavit for the purpose of determining the inheritance tax, were the following items of personal property which may be taxable under the Act of June 17, 1913, P. L. 507 and its amendments for county and city purposes:

DESCRIPTION	APPRAISED VALUE	DATE ACQUIRED BY DECEDENT

(If more space is needed, attach additional sheet of same size)

NOTE—A copy of the inventory, with the taxable items marked or indicated thereon, may be attached hereto and made a part of this affidavit

Deponent further avers that the items listed or indicated disclose all of the items of personal property of which decedent died possessed or in which decedent had any right, title or interest at the time of death, subject to a tax under the provisions of the said Act of June 17, 1913, P. L. 507 and its amendments to the best of deponent's knowledge and belief.

Sworn to and subscribed before me this
day of 19 .

. . . .

. . . .

Address of Executor or Administrator. . . . .

Name and Address of Attorney. . . . .

No..........................

..................................of 19

ESTATE OF

....
Deceased

Affidavit

AS TO PERSONAL PROPERTY

In compliance with the Act of May 13, 1917
(Act No. 610)

Filed..........................19

APPENDIX 18

Inventory

An inventory of the personal assets and real estate with valuation is filed by the executor or administrator with the probate court. Chapter 9 discusses types of assets and appraisals.

Commonwealth of Pennsylvania ⎰ SS:
Delaware County ⎱

**THIS FORM MUST BE
FILED IN TRIPLICATE**

If the decedent owned U. S. Savings Bonds
issued, jointly or otherwise,
submit list giving full information.

Execut
Adminstra   of the Estate of_____

deceased, verify (ies) that the statements contained in the following Inventory are true and
correct to the best of my (our) knowledge, information and belief. I (we) understand that
false statements herein are made subject to the penalties of 18 PaC.S. Section 4904, relating
to unsworn falsification to authorities. This inventory includes all of the personal assets
wherever situate and all of the real estate in the Commonwealth of Pennsylvania of said
decedent, that the valuation placed opposite each item of said Inventory represents its fair
value as of the date of the decedent's death, and that decedent owned no real estate outside
of the Commonwealth of Pennsylvania except that which appears in a memorandum at the end of
this Inventory.

_____

_____

INVENTORY

Of all the real and personal property of_____

late of_____ of _____ Delaware County, Pennsylvania, deceased

INVENTORY

WILL
ADM. No..........................

ESTATE OF

....

....

Deceased

Book..............................

Page..............................

Attorney

....

....

APPENDIX 19

Notice to Beneficiaries & Certification

This notice states the requirements for notification of beneficiaries and intestate heirs, information to be included with the notice and requirement for certification of notice. This is a Pennsylvania requirement and form. Other jurisdictions may have similar forms or requirements for notification.

SUPREME COURT RULE 5.6

NOTICE TO BENEFICIARIES AND INTESTATE HEIRS

(a) Requirement of notice. Within three (3) months after the grant of letters, the personal representative to whom original letters have been granted or his counsel shall send a written notice in substantially the form prescribed to:

(1) every person, corporation, association, entity or other party named in decedent's will as an outright beneficiary whether individually or as a class member;

(2) the appointed guardian of the estate, parent or legal custodian of any beneficiary who is a minor child under the age of 18 years;

(3) the appointed guardian of the estate or, in the absence of such appointment, the institution or person with custody of any beneficiary who is an adjudicated mental incompetent;

(4) the Attorney General on behalf of any charitable beneficiary whose interest exceeds $25,000 or which will not be paid in full;

(5) the Arrorney General on behalf of any governmental beneficiary or in default of the other heirs of the estate;

(6) the trustee of any trust which is a beneficiary; and

(7) the spouse, children or other intestate heirs of the decedent as determined under Chapter 21 of the Probate Estates and Fiduciaries Code.

(b) Contents of notice. The notice shall contain the following information:

(1) the date and place of decedents's death;

(2) whether decedent died testate or intestate;

(3) the county in which original letters were granted;

(4) the names, addresses and telephone numbers of all appointed personal representatives and their counsel; and

(5) a copy of the will or a description of the beneficiary's interest in the estate.

NOTICE OF BENEFICIAL INTEREST IN ESTATE

BEFORE THE REGISTER OF WILLS, COUNTY OF DELAWARE, PENNSYLVANIA

In re Estate of_____, deceased,

No. 23- -

TO:_____ (beneficiary)

_____ (address)

     Please take notice of the death of decedent and the grant of letters to the personal representative(s) named below. Your may have a beneficia interest in the estate as follows:

_____

_____

Name of decedent_____

Last know address of decedent_____

_____

Date of death_____, Place of death_____

County of grant of original letters_____

Decedent died_____testate _____intestate.

A copy of the will ___is ___is not attached.

Name(s), address(es) and telephone number(s) of all personal representatives appointed

Name   Address   Telephone

_____

_____

Names(s), address(es) and telephone number(s) of all counsel

Names   Address   Telephone

_____

_____

Additional information may be obtained from the undersigned.

Date_____   Signature_____

                          Name_____

Telephone_____   Address_____

Capacity:____Personal Representative _____

         ____Counsel for personal representative

CERTIFICATION OF NOTICE UNDER RULE 5.6(a)

Name of Decedent:_____

Date of Death:_____

File No._____

To the Register:

       I certify that notice of beneficial interest required by Rule 5.6 (a) of the Orphans' Court Rules was served on or mailed to the following beneficiaries of the above-captioned estate on
_____.
(date)

Name   Address

_____

_____

_____

_____

Notice has now been given to all persons entitled thereto under Rule 5.6(a) except_____

_____

Date:_____   _____
                              Signature

                              Name_____

                              Address_____

                              _____

                              Telephone(___)_____

                              Capacity:___Personal Representative

                              ___Counsel for Personal
                              Representative

APPENDIX 20

Status Report by Personal Representative

The requirement for reporting on the status of completion of administration and filing of accounting and form of Status Report. This is a Pennsylvania report. Determine the local requirements for filing.

RULE 6.12 STATUS REPORT
BY PERSONAL REPRESENTATIVE

(a) <u>Report of uncompleted administration</u>. If administration of an estate has not been completed within two years of the decedent's death, the personal representative or counsel shall file at such time, and annually thereafter until the administration is completed, a report with the Register of Wills showing the date by which the personal representative or counsel reasonably believes administration will be completed.

(b) <u>Report of completed administration</u>. Upon completion of the administration of an estate, the personal representative or his, her or its counsel shall file with the Register of Wills a report showing:

    (1) completion of administration of the estate;

    (2) whether a formal account was filed with the Orphans' Court;

    (3) whether a complete account was informally stated to all parties in interest;

    (4) whether final distribution has been completed; and

    (5) whether approvals of the account, receipts, joinders and releases have been filed with the Clerk of the Orphans' Court.

(c) <u>Form of report</u>. The report required by this Rule shall be in substantially the prescribed form.

(d) <u>No fee</u>. No fee shall be charged for filing the report required by this Rule.

(e) Copy of rule. Upon the grant of letters, the Register shall give a copy of this Rule to each personal representative and his, her or its counsel.

(f) <u>Failure to file a report</u>. After at least ten (10) days prior notice to a delinquent personal representative and counsel, the Clerk of the Orphans' Court shall inform the Court of the failure to file the report required by this Rule with a request that the Court conduct a hearing to determine what sanctions, if any, should be imposed.

APPENDIX 21

Letter to Legatee

The letter provides a format for notifying legatees that the estate is in position to pay a bequest and requiring receipt to the executor.

LETTER TO LEGATEE

LETTERHEAD

Date

Name
Address

Dear _____ :

    The Estate of _____ is now in a position
to pay to you the bequest left to you in his, her will in the amount of
$_____. I am enclosing a Receipt, Release and Refunding Bond. If you
will sign it and return it to me, as Executor of the Estate, I will then forward
to you promptly, a check in that amount in satisfaction of your bequest.

    Please contact me if there are any questions.

                                    Very truly yours,

                                    _____(signature)
                                    (typed name)
                                    Executor

APPENDIX 22

Receipt, Release and Refunding Bond and Receipt for Personal Property

Forms for receipt of cash and personal property, and release to the executor. The signature is notarized.

RECEIPT, RELEASE AND REFUNDING BOND

RE: ESTATE OF _____ DECEASED

     I, the undersigned _____(name) being an heir of the above captioned estate do hereby acknowledge that I have received from the estate jewelry and cash in total value of _____, as the net distributive share of said estate.

     I do hereby accept and receive the said amount with the same force and effect as if it had been scheduled in a First and Final Account filed in the Office of the Register of Wills and audited in the Orphans' Court of _____ County and had been adjudicated and confirmed absolutely and the amount paid to me had been awarded to me.

     And I do further agree, in consideration of the payment to me of the said amount, to refund to the said estate pro rata, any amount which may be necessary in the future to discharge any liabilities of the estate of which I may receive notice.

     IN WITNESS WHEREOF, I have hereunto set my hand and seal this _____ day of _____(month), 199_.

_____(SEAL)

STATE OF TEXAS   §

COUNTY OF BEXAR   §   RELEASE AND RECEIPT

      Now comes   the daughter of

, and acknowledges receipt of

"all tangible personal property" belonging to

      and bequeathed to me in the third paragraph

of her Will.

      With the receipt of all such property, I hereby release

the independent executor of this estate, FRANK W. BAUERS,

from any and all liability from, for, or stemming from the

ownership and possession of "all tangible personal property"

previously belonging to

      SIGNED this _15th_ day of _March_, 1982.

SUBSCRIBED AND SWORN TO before me this _15th_ day of

March, 1982.

NOTARY PUBLIC in and for
Bexar County, Texas

My commission expires: _____

JOHN C. ZINN
Notary Public, State of Texas
My commission expires 5-31-85

APPENDIX 23

Affidavit of Decedent's Legal Residence at Time of Death

An affidavit of domicile may be required by some companies prior to transfer of ownership of shares which were held by the decedent.

Company: Ameritech Account: 030-017-271
Inquiry Number: 060190-140421-0000

AFFIDAVIT OF DECEDENT'S LEGAL RESIDENCE AT TIME OF DEATH
FILED BY EXECUTOR/ADMINISTRATOR/SURVIVOR

State of _____

County of _____

_____

I,_____, being duly sworn, depose and say:
That I reside at _____
          City of _____
          State of _____
and am Executor/Administrator/Survivor of _____ deceased

who died on _____ _____ _____
                (Month)   (Day)   (Year)

_____

At the time of death the decedent was a resident of the State of _____
for _____ years.

     IMPORTANT: If less than 1 year, show former State of Residence

                    _____

At the time of death decedent was the owner of:

     a) _____ Share(s) of Common Stock
     b) _____ Shares of Nonconvertible Preferred Stock
     c) _____ Principal Amount of Debenture(s)

of American Information Technologies Corporation, a corporation organized under the laws
of the State of Delaware and, that at such time, the securities were physically located in
the City of _____, State of _____.
_____

Sworn to (or affirmed) before me
this _____ day of _____, 19_____

_____   _____
          Notary Public   (Sign here)

My Commission expires_____
(Affix Seal)

                                              FCC Item No. 6c

APPENDIX 24

Suggested Accounting Formats

These forms may be used to record the collection of assets and income, expenses and distribution and for first and final accounting. You may design your own forms or use your PC for recording, or your accountant or attorney may have a format which they use. The important factor is to record everything that comes in to the estate or is paid out and to be able to account for it to the probate court and to the beneficiaries.

COLLECTION OF ASSETS AND INCOME

| SOURCE | DATE | DEPOSIT AMOUNT | DATE OF DEP. | ASSETS | | | | | INCOME | | | |
				CHECKING ACCOUNTS	BANK & SAVINGS ACCOUNTS	SECURITIES SALES	INSURANCE PROCEEDS	SETTLEMENT PROCEEDS	OTHER	DIVIDENDS	INTEREST	RECEIPTS

EXPENSE & DISTRIBUTIONS

DATE	PAYEE	CHECK NO.	TOTAL AMT.	ADMIN & TRAVEL	DEBTS	TAXES	PROPERTY MAINT.	FUNERAL EXPENSE	OTHER EXPENSE	APPRAISALS	BEQUESTS	DISTRIBUTIONS	EXPLANATION

FORMAT FOR ACCOUNTING

FIRST AND FINAL ACCOUNT OF

_____, EXECUTOR

FOR

ESTATE OF _____

DATE OF DEATH:

DATE OF EXECUTOR'S APPOINTMENT:

DATE OF FIRST ADVERTISEMENT OF
    GRANT OF LETTERS:

ACCOUNTING FOR THE PERIOD:

PURPOSE OF ACCOUNT: _____, EXECUTOR, offers this account to acquaint interested parties with the transactions that have occurred during his administration. The account also indicates the proposed distribution of the estate.

It is important that the account be carefully examined - Requests for additional information or questions or objections can be discussed with:

Name of Executor or Counsel

RECEIPTS OF PRINCIPAL

Assets Listed in Inventory

CASH:

List accounts and balances $

_____

STOCKS and BONDS

List Number of shares, company and value $

_____   _____

TOTAL INVENTORY $

RECEIPTS SUBSEQUENT TO INVENTORY

List proceeds of sale of real estate
Insurance refunds
Other receipts   _____

$_____

Total Receipts of Principal $_____

GAINS AND LOSSES ON SALES OR OTHER DISPOSITIONS

	GAIN	LOSS
Net Proceeds		
Fiduciary Acquisition Value _____		
(List each sale or disposition)		
	_____	_____
TOTAL GAINS AND LOSSES	$ _____	$ _____
Less Loss	_____	
Net Gain (or Loss)	$_____	

DISBURSEMENTS OF PRINCIPAL

Debts of Decedent $

(List debts) _____

Funeral Expenses _____

Family Exemption _____

Administration Expenses _____

Federal and State Taxes _____

Fees and Commissions _____ _____

Total $_____

Distributions of Principal to Beneficiaries

List legacies and distributions _____

Total Distributions of Principal to Beneficiaries $_____

Principal Balance on Hand

Name of institution and type of account _____

$_____

Receipts of Income

Dividends $ _____

Interest   _____ $_____

Disbursement of Income

List Disbursements $ _____ $_____

Distributions of Income to Beneficiaries

List Distributions $ _____ $_____

Proposed Distribution to Beneficiaries

List Beneficiaries and Amounts $ _____ $_____

**Reserve Required for Payment of
Taxes and Filing Account** $_____

_____, Executor, under the Last Will and Testament of _____, deceased, hereby declares under oath (penalties of perjury) that he has fully and faithfully discharged the duties of his office; that the foregoing First and Final Account is true and correct and fully discloses all significant transactions occurring during the accounting period; that all known claims against the estate have been paid in full; that to his knowledge, there are no claims now outstanding against the estate and that all taxes presently due from the estate have been paid.

_____(signature)

(typed name)
Executor

SUBSCRIBED AND AFFIRMED
By
before me this   day
of

_____
NOTARY PUBLIC

APPENDIX 25

Form 1041, U.S. Income Tax Return For Estates and Trusts and Schedule K-1

Form 1041 is used for filing federal income tax returns for estates and trusts. Form K-1 is attached to the 1041 and a copy of the K-1 is sent to the beneficiary.

Form **1041**	Department of the Treasury — Internal Revenue Service **U.S. Income Tax Return for Estates and Trusts**	**1997**

For calendar year 1997 or fiscal year beginning , 1997, and ending , 19 | OMB No. 1545-0092

A Type of entity:
- ☐ Decedent's estate
- ☐ Simple trust
- ☐ Complex trust
- ☐ Grantor type trust
- ☐ Bankruptcy estate-Ch. 7
- ☐ Bankruptcy estate-Ch. 11
- ☐ Pooled income fund

B Number of Schedules K-1 attached (see instructions) ▶

Name of estate or trust (If a grantor type trust, see page 8 of the instructions.)

Name and title of fiduciary

Number, street, and room or suite no. (If a P.O. box, see page 8 of the instructions.)

City or town, state, and ZIP code

C Employer identification number

D Date entity created

E Nonexempt charitable and split-interest trusts, check applicable boxes (see page 10 of the instructions):
- ☐ Described in section 4947(a)(1)
- ☐ Not a private foundation
- ☐ Described in section 4947(a)(2)

F Check applicable boxes:
- ☐ Initial return
- ☐ Final return
- ☐ Amended return
- ☐ Change in fiduciary's name
- ☐ Change in fiduciary's address

G Pooled mortgage account (see page 10 of the instructions):
- ☐ Bought
- ☐ Sold
- Date:

Income

1	Interest income	1
2	Dividends	2
3	Business income or (loss) (attach Schedule C or C-EZ (Form 1040))	3
4	Capital gain or (loss) (attach Schedule D (Form 1041))	4
5	Rents, royalties, partnerships, other estates and trusts, etc. (attach Schedule E (Form 1040))	5
6	Farm income or (loss) (attach Schedule F (Form 1040))	6
7	Ordinary gain or (loss) (attach Form 4797)	7
8	Other income. List type and amount _____	8
9	**Total income.** Combine lines 1 through 8 ▶	9

Deductions

10	Interest. Check if Form 4952 is attached ▶ ☐	10
11	Taxes	11
12	Fiduciary fees	12
13	Charitable deduction (from Schedule A, line 7)	13
14	Attorney, accountant, and return preparer fees	14
15a	Other deductions NOT subject to the 2% floor (attach schedule)	15a
b	Allowable miscellaneous itemized deductions subject to the 2% floor	15b
16	**Total.** Add lines 10 through 15b	16
17	Adjusted total income or (loss). Subtract line 16 from line 9. Enter here and on Schedule B, line 1 ▶	17
18	Income distribution deduction (from Schedule B, line 15) (attach Schedules K-1 (Form 1041))	18
19	Estate tax deduction (including certain generation-skipping taxes) (attach computation)	19
20	Reserved	20
21	Exemption	21
22	**Total deductions.** Add lines 18, 19, and 21 ▶	22

Tax and Payments

23	Taxable income. Subtract line 22 from line 17. If a loss, see page 14 of the instructions	23
24	**Total tax** (from Schedule G, line 8)	24
25	**Payments: a** 1997 estimated tax payments and amount applied from 1996 return	25a
b	Estimated tax payments allocated to beneficiaries (from Form 1041-T)	25b
c	Subtract line 25b from line 25a	25c
d	Tax paid with extension of time to file: ☐ Form 2758 ☐ Form 8736 ☐ Form 8800	25d
e	Federal income tax withheld. If any is from Form(s) 1099, check ▶ ☐	25e
	Other payments: **f** Form 2439 _____ ; **g** Form 4136 _____ ; Total ▶	25h
26	**Total payments.** Add lines 25c through 25e, and 25h ▶	26
27	Estimated tax penalty (see page 15 of the instructions)	27
28	**Tax due.** If line 26 is smaller than the total of lines 24 and 27, enter amount owed	28
29	**Overpayment.** If line 26 is larger than the total of lines 24 and 27, enter amount overpaid	29
30	Amount of line 29 to be: **a Credited to 1998 estimated tax** ▶ ; **b Refunded** ▶	30

Please Sign Here

Under penalties of perjury, I declare that I have examined this return, including accompanying schedules and statements, and to the best of my knowledge and belief, it is true, correct, and complete. Declaration of preparer (other than fiduciary) is based on all information of which preparer has any knowledge.

▶ _____ Signature of fiduciary or officer representing fiduciary | Date | ▶ _____ EIN of fiduciary if a financial institution (see page 5 of the instructions)

Paid Preparer's Use Only

Preparer's signature ▶	Date	Check if self-employed ▶ ☐	Preparer's social security no.
Firm's name (or yours if self-employed) and address ▶		EIN ▶	
		ZIP code ▶	

For Paperwork Reduction Act Notice, see the separate instructions. ISA

Form **1041** (1997)

STF FED3211F.1

Schedule A	**Charitable Deduction.** Do not complete for a simple trust or a pooled income fund.		
1	Amounts paid or permanently set aside for charitable purposes from gross income (see page 15) .	**1**	
2	Tax-exempt income allocable to charitable contributions (see page 16 of the instructions)	**2**	
3	Subtract line 2 from line 1	**3**	
4	Capital gains for the tax year allocated to corpus and paid or permanently set aside for charitable purposes	**4**	
5	Add lines 3 and 4	**5**	
6	Section 1202 exclusion allocable to capital gains paid or permanently set aside for charitable purposes (see page 16 of the instructions)	**6**	
7	**Charitable deduction.** Subtract line 6 from 5. Enter here and on page 1, line 13	**7**	

Schedule B	**Income Distribution Deduction**		
1	Adjusted total income (from page 1, line 17) (see page 16 of the instructions)	**1**	
2	Adjusted tax-exempt interest	**2**	
3	Total net gain from Schedule D (Form 1041), line 16, column (1) (see page 16 of the instructions) .	**3**	
4	Enter amount from Schedule A, line 4 (reduced by any allocable section 1202 exclusion)	**4**	
5	Capital gains for the tax year included on Schedule A, line 1 (see page 16 of the instructions) . . .	**5**	
6	Enter any gain from page 1, line 4, as a negative number. If page 1, line 4, is a loss, enter the loss as a positive number	**6**	
7	**Distributable net income (DNI).** Combine lines 1 through 6. If zero or less, enter -0-	**7**	
8	If a complex trust, enter accounting income for the tax year as determined under the governing instrument and applicable local law . . **8**		
9	Income required to be distributed currently	**9**	
10	Other amounts paid, credited, or otherwise required to be distributed	**10**	
11	Total distributions. Add lines 9 and 10. If greater than line 8, see page 17 of the instructions	**11**	
12	Enter the amount of tax-exempt income included on line 11	**12**	
13	Tentative income distribution deduction. Subtract line 12 from line 11	**13**	
14	Tentative income distribution deduction. Subtract line 2 from line 7. If zero or less, enter -0-	**14**	
15	**Income distribution deduction.** Enter the smaller of line 13 or line 14 here and on page 1, line 18	**15**	

Schedule G	**Tax Computation** (see page 17 of the instructions)			
1	**Tax: a** ☐ Tax rate schedule or ☐ Schedule D (Form 1041)	**1a**		
	b Other taxes	**1b**		
	c Total. Add lines 1a and 1b . . . . ▶		**1c**	
2a	Foreign tax credit (attach Form 1116)	**2a**		
b	Check: ☐ Nonconventional source fuel credit ☐ Form 8834 . . .	**2b**		
c	General business credit. Enter here and check which forms are attached:			
	☐ Form 3800 or ☐ Forms (specify) ▶ _____	**2c**		
	d Credit for prior year minimum tax (attach Form 8801)	**2d**		
3	**Total credits.** Add lines 2a through 2d . . . . ▶		**3**	
4	Subtract line 3 from line 1c		**4**	
5	Recapture taxes. Check if from: ☐ Form 4255 ☐ Form 8611		**5**	
6	Alternative minimum tax (from Schedule I, line 42)		**6**	
7	Household employment taxes. Attach Schedule H (Form 1040) . . . . ▶		**7**	
8	**Total tax.** Add lines 4 through 7. Enter here and on page 1, line 24		**8**	

	Other Information	Yes	No
1	Did the estate or trust receive tax-exempt income? If "Yes," attach a computation of the allocation of expenses. . . . . Enter the amount of tax-exempt interest income and exempt-interest dividends ▶ $ _____		
2	Did the estate or trust receive all or any part of the earnings (salary, wages, and other compensation) of any individual by reason of a contract assignment or similar arrangement?		
3	At any time during calendar year 1997, did the estate or trust have an interest in or a signature or other authority over a bank, securities, or other financial account in a foreign country? See page 19 of the instructions for exceptions and filing requirements for Form TD F 90-22.1. If "Yes," enter the name of the foreign country ▶ _____		
4	During the tax year, did the estate or trust receive a distribution from, or was it the grantor of, or transferor to, a foreign trust? If "Yes," the estate or trust may have to file Form 3520 or 926. See page 19 of the instructions		
5	Did the estate or trust receive, or pay, any seller-financed mortgage interest? If "Yes," see page 19 for required attachment		
6	If this is an estate or a complex trust making the section 663(b) election, check here (see page 19) . . . . ▶ ☐		
7	To make a section 643(e)(3) election, attach Schedule D (Form 1041), and check here (see page 19) . . . . . . ▶ ☐		
8	If the decedent's estate has been open for more than 2 years, check here . . . . ▶ ☐		
9	Are any trust beneficiaries skip persons? See page 19 of the instructions		

STF FED3211F.2

Schedule I	Alternative Minimum Tax (see pages 19 through 24 of the instructions)

Part I — Estate's or Trust's Share of Alternative Minimum Taxable Income

1	Adjusted total income or (loss) (from page 1, line 17)	**1**	
2	Net operating loss deduction. Enter as a positive amount	**2**	
3	Add lines 1 and 2	**3**	
4	**Adjustments and tax preference items:**		

a	Interest	**4a**	
b	Taxes	**4b**	
c	Miscellaneous itemized deductions (from page 1, line 15b)	**4c**	
d	Refund of taxes	**4d** ( )	
e	Depreciation of property placed in service after 1986	**4e**	
f	Circulation and research and experimental expenditures	**4f**	
g	Mining exploration and development costs	**4g**	
h	Long-term contracts entered into after February 28, 1986	**4h**	
i	Amortization of pollution control facilities	**4i**	
j	Installment sales of certain property	**4j**	
k	Adjusted gain or loss (including incentive stock options)	**4k**	
l	Certain loss limitations	**4l**	
m	Tax shelter farm activities	**4m**	
n	Passive activities	**4n**	
o	Beneficiaries of other trusts or decedent's estates	**4o**	
p	Tax-exempt interest from specified private activity bonds	**4p**	
q	Depletion	**4q**	
r	Accelerated depreciation of real property placed in service before 1987	**4r**	
s	Accelerated depreciation of leased personal property placed in service before 1987	**4s**	
t	Intangible drilling costs	**4t**	
u	Other adjustments	**4u**	

5	Combine lines 4a through 4u	**5**	
6	Add lines 3 and 5	**6**	
7	Alternative tax net operating loss deduction (see page 23 of the instructions for limitations)	**7**	
8	Adjusted alternative minimum taxable income. Subtract line 7 from line 6. Enter here and on line 14	**8**	

Note: *Complete Part II below before going to line 9.*

9	Income distribution deduction from line 28 below	**9**	
10	Estate tax deduction (from page 1, line 19)	**10**	
11	Reserved	**11**	
12	Add lines 9 and 10	**12**	
13	Estate's or trust's share of alternative minimum taxable income. Subtract line 12 from line 8	**13**	

If line 13 is:

- $22,500 or less, stop here and enter -0- on Schedule G, line 6. The estate or trust is not liable for the alternative minimum tax.
- Over $22,500, but less than $165,000, go to line 29.
- $165,000 or more, enter the amount from line 13 on line 35 and go to line 36.

Part II — Income Distribution Deduction on a Minimum Tax Basis

14	Adjusted alternative minimum taxable income (from line 8)	**14**	
15	Adjusted tax-exempt interest (other than amounts included on line 4p)	**15**	
16	Total net gain from Schedule D (Form 1041), line 16, column (1). If a loss, enter -0-	**16**	
17	Capital gains for the tax year allocated to corpus and paid or permanently set aside for charitable purposes (from Schedule A, line 4) . .	**17**	
18	Capital gains paid or permanently set aside for charitable purposes from gross income (see page 23 of the instructions)	**18**	
19	Capital gains computed on a minimum tax basis included on line 8	**19** ( )	
20	Capital losses computed on a minimum tax basis included on line 8. Enter as a positive amount .	**20**	
21	Distributable net alternative minimum taxable income (DNAMTI). Combine lines 14 through 20. If zero or less, enter -0-	**21**	
22	Income required to be distributed currently (from Schedule B, line 9)	**22**	
23	Other amounts paid, credited, or otherwise required to be distributed (from Schedule B, line 10) .	**23**	
24	Total distributions. Add lines 22 and 23	**24**	
25	Tax-exempt income included on line 24 (other than amounts included on line 4p)	**25**	
26	Tentative income distribution deduction on a minimum tax basis. Subtract line 25 from line 24. . .	**26**	
27	Tentative income distribution deduction on a minimum tax basis. Subtract line 15 from line 21. If zero or less, enter -0-	**27**	
28	**Income distribution deduction on a minimum tax basis.** Enter the smaller of line 26 or line 27. Enter here and on line 9	**28**	

Part III — Alternative Minimum Tax

29	Exemption amount		**29**	$22,500
30	Enter the amount from line 13	**30**		
31	Phase-out of exemption amount	**31**	$75,000	
32	Subtract line 31 from line 30. If zero or less, enter -0-	**32**		
33	Multiply line 32 by 25% (.25)			**33**	
34	Subtract line 33 from line 29. If zero or less, enter -0-		**34**	
35	Subtract line 34 from line 30		**35**	
36	If the estate or trust completed Schedule D (Form 1041) and had an amount on line 24 or 27 (as refigured for the AMT, if necessary), go to Part IV to figure line 36. **All others:** If line 35 is — ● $175,000 or less, multiply line 35 by 26% (.26). ● Over $175,000, multiply line 35 by 28% (.28) and subtract $3,500 from the result		**36**	
37	Alternative minimum foreign tax credit (see page 24 of instructions)		**37**	
38	Tentative minimum tax. Subtract line 37 from line 36		**38**	
39	Regular tax before credits (see page 24 of instructions)	**39**		
40	Section 644 tax included on Schedule G, line 1b	**40**		
41	Add lines 39 and 40		**41**	
42	**Alternative minimum tax.** Subtract line 41 from line 38. If zero or less, enter -0-. Enter here and on Schedule G, line 6		**42**	

Part IV — Line 36 Computation Using Maximum Capital Gains Rates

43	Enter the amount from line 35		**43**	
44	Enter the amount from Schedule D (Form 1041), line 27 (as refigured for AMT, if necessary)	**44**		
45	Enter the amount from Schedule D (Form 1041), line 24 (as refigured for AMT, if necessary)	**45**		
46	Add lines 44 and 45. If zero or less, enter -0-	**46**		
47	Enter the amount from Schedule D (Form 1041), line 21 (as refigured for AMT, if necessary)	**47**		
48	Enter the **smaller** of line 46 or line 47		**48**	
49	Subtract line 48 from line 43. If zero or less, enter -0-		**49**	
50	If line 49 is $175,000 or less, multiply line 49 by 26% (.26). Otherwise, multiply line 49 by 28% (.28) and subtract $3,500 from the result . . . . ▶		**50**	
51	Enter the amount from Schedule D (Form 1041), line 36 (as figured for the regular tax)		**51**	
52	Enter the **smallest** of line 43, line 44, or line 51		**52**	
53	Multiply line 52 by 10% (.10) . . . . ▶		**53**	
54	Enter the **smaller** of line 43 or line 44		**54**	
55	Enter the amount from line 52		**55**	
56	Subtract line 55 from line 54. If zero or less, enter -0- . . . . ▶		**56**	
57	Multiply line 56 by 20% (.20)		**57**	
58	Enter the amount from line 43		**58**	
59	Add lines 49, 52, and 56		**59**	
60	Subtract line 59 from line 58		**60**	
61	Multiply line 60 by 25% (.25) . . . . ▶		**61**	
62	Add lines 50, 53, 57, and 61		**62**	
63	If line 43 is $175,000 or less, multiply line 43 by 26% (.26). Otherwise, multiply line 43 by 28% (.28) and subtract $3,500 from the result . . . . ▶		**63**	
64	Enter the **smaller** of line 62 or line 63 here and on line 36 . . . . ▶		**64**	

SCHEDULE D
(Form 1041)

Department of the Treasury
Internal Revenue Service

Capital Gains and Losses

▶ Attach to Form 1041 (or Form 5227). See the separate instructions for
Form 1041 (or Form 5227).

OMB No. 1545-0092

1997

Name of estate or trust

Employer identification number

Note: *Form 5227 filers need to complete ONLY Parts I and II.*

Part I	**Short-Term Capital Gains and Losses — Assets Held One Year or Less**

(a) Description of property (Example, 100 shares 7% preferred of "Z" Co.)	(b) Date acquired (mo., day, yr.)	(c) Date sold (mo., day, yr.)	(d) Sales price	(e) Cost or other basis (see page 26)	(f) Gain or (loss) for entire year. (col. (d) less col. (e))	
1						

2	Short-term capital gain or (loss) from Forms 4684, 6252, 6781, and 8824	**2**	
3	Net short-term gain or (loss) from partnerships, S corporations, and other estates or trusts	**3**	
4	Short-term capital loss carryover from 1996 Schedule D, line 28	**4** ( )	
5	**Net short-term gain or (loss).** Combine lines 1 through 4 in column (f). Enter here and on line 14 below . . . . ▶	**5**	

Part II	**Long-Term Capital Gains and Losses — Assets Held More Than One Year**

(a) Description of property (Example, 100 shares 7% preferred of "Z" Co.)	(b) Date acquired (mo., day, yr.)	(c) Date sold (mo., day, yr.)	(d) Sales price	(e) Cost or other basis (see page 26)	(f) Gain or (loss) for entire year. (col. (d) less col. (e))	(g) 28% rate gain or (loss) *(see instr. below)
6						

7	Long-term capital gain or (loss) from Forms 2439, 4684, 6252, 6781, and 8824	**7**	
8	Net long-term gain or (loss) from partnerships, S corporations, and other estates or trusts	**8**	
9	Capital gain distributions	**9**	
10	Gain from Form 4797, Part I	**10**	
11	Long-term capital loss carryover. Enter in both columns (f) and (g) the amount, if any, from 1996 Schedule D, line 35	**11** ( ) ( )	
12	Combine lines 6 through 11 in column (g)	**12**	
13	**Net long-term gain or (loss).** Combine lines 6 through 11 in column (f). Enter here and on line 15 below . . . . ▶	**13**	

***28% rate gain or (loss)** includes all gains and losses in Part II, column (f) from sales, exchanges, or conversions (including installment payments received) **either:**
- **Before** May 7, 1997, **or**
- **After** July 28, 1997, for assets held more than 1 year but **not** more than 18 months.

It also includes **ALL** "collectibles gains and losses" (as defined on page 26 of the instructions) and the taxable gain (but not more than the section 1202 exclusion) on the sale or exchange of qualified small business stock.

Part III	**Summary of Parts I and II**		**(1)** Beneficiaries' (see page 27)	**(2)** Estate's or trust's	**(3)** Total
14	**Net short-term gain or (loss)** (from line 5 above)	**14**			
15	**Net long-term gain or (loss):**				
a	28% rate gain or (loss) (from line 12 above)	**15a**			
b	Unrecaptured section 1250 gain (see page 27 of the instructions)	**15b**			
c	Total for year (from line 13 above)	**15c**			
16	**Total net gain or (loss).** Combine lines 14 and 15c . . . . . ▶	**16**			

Note: *If line 16, column (3), is a net gain, enter the gain on Form 1041, line 4. If lines 15c and 16, column (2) are net gains, go to Part V, and DO NOT complete Part IV. If line 16, column (3), is a net loss, complete Part IV and the* **Capital Loss Carryover Worksheet,** *as necessary.*

For Paperwork Reduction Act Notice, see the Instructions for Form 1041.

Schedule D (Form 1041) 1997

| **Part IV** | **Capital Loss Limitation** |

17   Enter here and enter as a (loss) on Form 1041, line 4, the **smaller** of:

   a   The loss on line 16, column (3); **or**

   b $3,000 . . . .   **17** (   )

*If the loss on line 16, column (3) is more than $3,000, OR if Form 1041, page 1, line 23, is a loss, complete the **Capital Loss Carryover Worksheet** on page 27 of the instructions to determine your capital loss carryover.*

| **Part V** | **Tax Computation Using Maximum Capital Gains Rates** (Complete this part **only** if both lines 15c and 16 in column (2) are gains, and Form 1041, line 23 is more than zero.) |

18   Enter taxable income from Form 1041, line 23 . . . .   **18**

19   Enter the **smaller** of line 15c or 16 in column (2) **19**

20   If you are filing Form 4952, enter the amount from Form 4952, line 4e . . .   **20**

21   Subtract line 20 from line 19. If zero or less, enter -0- **21**

22   Combine lines 14 and 15a, column (2). If zero or less, enter -0- **22**

23   Enter the **smaller** of line 15a, column (2), or line 22, but not less than zero   **23**

24   Enter the amount from line 15b, column (2) **24**

25   Reserved **25**

26   Add lines 23 and 24 . . . .   **26**

27   Subtract line 26 from line 21. If zero or less, enter -0- **27**

28   Subtract line 27 from line 18. If zero or less, enter -0- **28**

29   Enter the **smaller** of line 18 or $1,650 . . . .   **29**

30   Enter the **smaller** of line 28 or line 29 . . . .   **30**

31   Subtract line 21 from line 18. If zero or less, enter -0- **31**

32   Enter the **larger** of line 30 or line 31 . . . .   **32**

33   Tax on amount on line 32 from the 1997 Tax Rate Schedule . . . . ▶   **33**

34   Enter the amount from line 29 . . . .   **34**

35   Enter the amount from line 28 . . . .   **35**

36   Subtract line 35 from line 34. If zero or less, enter -0- **36**

37   Multiply line 36 by 10% (.10) . . . . ▶   **37**

38   Enter the **smaller** of line 18 or line 27 . . . .   **38**

39   Enter the amount from line 36 . . . .   **39**

40   Subtract line 39 from line 38. If zero or less, enter -0- **40**

41   Multiply line 40 by 20% (.20) . . . . ▶   **41**

42   Enter the **smaller** of line 21 or line 24 . . . .   **42**

43   Add lines 21 and 32 . . . .   **43**

44   Enter the amount from line 18 . . . .   **44**

45   Subtract line 44 from line 43. If zero or less, enter -0- **45**

46   Subtract line 45 from line 42. If zero or less, enter -0- **46**

47   Multiply line 46 by 25% (.25) . . . . ▶   **47**

48   Enter the amount from line 18 . . . .   **48**

49   Add lines 32, 36, 40, and 46 . . . .   **49**

50   Subtract line 49 from line 48 . . . .   **50**

51   Multiply line 50 by 28% (.28) . . . . ▶   **51**

52   Add lines 33, 37, 41, 47, and 51 . . . .   **52**

53   Tax on the amount on line 18 from the 1997 Tax Rate Schedule **53**

54   **Tax.** Enter the **smaller** of line 52 or line 53 here and on line 1a of Schedule G, Form 1041 . . . . . . ▶   **54**

SCHEDULE K-1
(Form 1041)

Department of the Treasury
Internal Revenue Service

Beneficiary's Share of Income, Deductions, Credits, etc.
for the calendar year 1997, or fiscal year
beginning _____ , 1997, ending _____ , 19 _____
▶ Complete a separate Schedule K-1 for each beneficiary.

OMB No. 1545-0092

1997

Name of trust or decedent's estate

☐ Amended K-1
☐ Final K-1

Beneficiary's identifying number ▶

Beneficiary's name, address, and ZIP code

Estate's or trust's EIN ▶

Fiduciary's name, address, and ZIP code

(a) Allocable share item		(b) Amount	(c) Calendar year 1997 Form 1040 filers enter the amounts in column (b) on:
1	Interest	1		Schedule B, Part I, line 1
2	Dividends...............................	2		Schedule B, Part II, line 5
3	Net short-term capital gain	3		Schedule D, line 5
4	Net long-term capital gain: **a** 28% rate gain	4a		Schedule D, line 12, column (g)
b	Unrecaptured section 1250 gain	4b		See the instructions for Schedule D, line 25
c	Total for year	4c		Schedule D, line 12, column (f)
5a	Annuities, royalties, and other nonpassive income before directly apportioned deductions	5a		Schedule E, Part III, column (f)
b	Depreciation...............................	5b		
c	Depletion	5c		Include on the applicable line of the appropriate tax form
d	Amortization..............................	5d		
6a	Trade or business, rental real estate, and other rental income before directly apportioned deductions (see instructions)	6a		Schedule E, Part III
b	Depreciation...............................	6b		
c	Depletion	6c		Include on the applicable line of the appropriate tax form
d	Amortization..............................	6d		
7	Income for minimum tax purposes	7		
8	Income for regular tax purposes (add lines 1, 2, 3, 4c, 5a, and 6a)	8		
9	Adjustment for minimum tax purposes (subtract line 8 from line 7)	9		Form 6251, line 12
10	Estate tax deduction (including certain generation-skipping transfer taxes)...............	10		Schedule A, line 27
11	Foreign taxes	11		Form 1116 or Schedule A (Form 1040), line 8
12	Adjustments and tax preference items (itemize):			
a	Accelerated depreciation	12a		
b	Depletion	12b		Include on the applicable line of Form 6251
c	Amortization..............................	12c		
d	Exclusion items	12d		1998 Form 8801
13	Deductions in the final year of trust or decedent's estate:			
a	Excess deductions on termination (see instructions) ..	13a		Schedule A, line 22
b	Short-term capital loss carryover	13b	( )	Schedule D, line 5
c	Long-term capital loss carryover	13c	( )	Schedule D, line 12, columns (f) and (g)
d	Net operating loss (NOL) carryover for regular tax purposes	13d	( )	Form 1040, line 21
e	NOL carryover for minimum tax purposes	13e		See the instructions for Form 6251, line 20
f	_____	13f		Include on the applicable line
g	_____	13g		of the appropriate tax form
14	Other (itemize):			
a	Payments of estimated taxes credited to you	14a		Form 1040, line 55
b	Tax-exempt interest	14b		Form 1040, line 8b
c	_____	14c		
d	_____	14d		
e	_____	14e		Include on the applicable line
f	_____	14f		of the appropriate tax form
g	_____	14g		
h	_____	14h		

For Paperwork Reduction Act Notice, see the Instructions for Form 1041.

ISA

Schedule K-1 (Form 1041) 1997

STF FED3219F.1

Instructions for Beneficiary Filing Form 1040

Note: *The fiduciary's instructions for completing Schedule K-1 are in the Instructions for Form 1041.*

General Instructions

Purpose of Form

The fiduciary of a trust or decedent's estate uses Schedule K-1 to report your share of the trust's or estate's income, credits, deductions, etc. **Keep it for your records. Do not file it with your tax return.** A copy has been filed with the IRS.

Inconsistent Treatment of Items

Generally, you must report items shown on your Schedule K-1 (and any attached schedules) the same way that the estate or trust treated the items on its return.

If the treatment on your original or amended return is inconsistent with the estate's or trust's treatment, or if the estate or trust was required to but has not filed a return, you must file **Form 8082,** Notice of Inconsistent Treatment or Administrative Adjustment Request (AAR), with your original or amended return to identify and explain any inconsistency (or to note that an estate or trust return has not been filed).

If you are required to file Form 8082 but fail to do so, you may be subject to the accuracy-related penalty. This penalty is in addition to any tax that results from making your amount or treatment of the item consistent with that shown on the estate's or trust's return. Any deficiency that results from making the amounts consistent may be assessed immediately.

Errors

If you believe the fiduciary has made an error on your Schedule K-1, notify the fiduciary and ask for an amended or a corrected Schedule K-1. **Do not** change any items on your copy. Be sure that the fiduciary sends a copy of the amended Schedule K-1 to the IRS. **If you are unable to reach agreement with the fiduciary regarding the inconsistency, you must file Form 8082.**

Tax Shelters

If you receive a copy of **Form 8271,** Investor Reporting of Tax Shelter Registration Number, see the instructions for Form 8271 to determine your reporting requirements.

Beneficiaries of Generation-Skipping Trusts

If you received **Form 706-GS(D-1),** Notification of Distribution From a Generation-Skipping Trust, and paid a generation-skipping transfer (GST) tax on **Form 706-GS(D),** Generation-Skipping Transfer Tax Return for Distributions, you can deduct the GST tax paid on income distributions on Schedule A (Form 1040), line 8. To figure the deduction, see the instructions for Form 706-GS(D).

Specific Instructions

Lines 3 and 4

If there is an attachment to this Schedule K-1 reporting a disposition of a passive activity, see the instructions for **Form 8582,** Passive Activity Loss Limitations, for information on the treatment of dispositions of interests in a passive activity.

Lines 6b through 6d

The deductions on lines 6b through 6d may be subject to the passive loss limitations of Internal Revenue Code section 469, which generally limits deductions from passive activities to the income from those activities. The rules for applying these limitations to beneficiaries have not yet been issued. For more details, see **Pub. 925,** Passive Activity and At-Risk Rules.

Line 12d

If you pay alternative minimum tax in 1997, the amount on line 12d will help you figure any minimum tax credit for 1998. See the 1998 **Form 8801,** Credit for Prior Year Minimum Tax — Individuals, Estates, and Trusts, for more information.

Line 14a

To figure any underpayment and penalty on **Form 2210,** Underpayment of Estimated Tax by Individuals, Estates, and Trusts, treat the amount entered on line 14a as an estimated tax payment made on January 15, 1998.

Lines 14c through 14h

The amount of gross farming and fishing income is included on line 6a. This income is also separately stated on line 14 to help you determine if you are subject to a penalty for underpayment of estimated tax. Report the amount of gross farming and fishing income on Schedule E (Form 1040), line 41.

APPENDIX 26

Inheritance Tax Return, Commonwealth of Pennsylvania, Including Schedules

The Pennsylvania Inheritance Tax Return and Schedules are included to indicate the range of data which must be accumulated and reported upon. It can serve as a guide during the performance of duties of the administrator or executor. The accountant or attorney who prepares the form will require the data in order to complete the report.

REV-1500 EX+ (7-94)

COMMONWEALTH OF PENNSYLVANIA
DEPARTMENT OF REVENUE
DEPT. 280601
HARRISBURG, PA 17128-0601

INHERITANCE TAX RETURN
RESIDENT DECEDENT
(TO BE FILED IN DUPLICATE
WITH REGISTER OF WILLS)

**FOR DATES OF DEATH AFTER 12/31/91 CHECK HERE
IF A SPOUSAL
POVERTY CREDIT IS CLAIMED** ☐

FILE NUMBER

COUNTY CODE	YEAR	NUMBER

DECEDENT

DECEDENT'S NAME (LAST, FIRST, AND MIDDLE INITIAL)

DECEDENT'S COMPLETE ADDRESS

SOCIAL SECURITY NUMBER | DATE OF DEATH | DATE OF BIRTH

County

(IF APPLICABLE) SURVIVING SPOUSE'S NAME (LAST, FIRST AND MIDDLE INITIAL) | SOCIAL SECURITY NUMBER | AMOUNT RECEIVED (SEE INSTRUCTIONS)

CHECK APPROPRIATE BLOCKS

☐ 1. Original Return

☐ 2. Supplemental Return

☐ 3. Remainder Return
(for dates of death prior to 12-13-82)

☐ 4. Limited Estate

☐ 4a. Future Interest Compromise
(for dates of death after 12-12-82)

☐ 5. Federal Estate Tax Return Required

☐ 6. Decedent Died Testate
(Attach copy of Will)

☐ 7. Decedent Maintained a Living Trust
(Attach copy of Trust)

___ 8. Total Number of Safe Deposit Boxes

CORRES-PONDENT

ALL CORRESPONDENCE AND CONFIDENTIAL TAX INFORMATION SHOULD BE DIRECTED TO:

NAME

COMPLETE MAILING ADDRESS

TELEPHONE NUMBER

( )

RECAPITULATION

1. Real Estate (Schedule A) (1) _____

2. Stocks and Bonds (Schedule B) (2) _____

3. Closely Held Stock/Partnership Interest (Schedule C) (3) _____

4. Mortgages and Notes Receivable (Schedule D) (4) _____

5. Cash, Bank Deposits & Miscellaneous Personal Property
(Schedule E) (5) _____

6. Jointly Owned Property (Schedule F) (6) _____

7. Transfers (Schedule G) (Schedule L) (7) _____

8. Total Gross Assets (total Lines 1-7) (8) _____

9. Funeral Expenses, Administrative Costs, Miscellaneous
Expenses (Schedule H) (9) _____

10. Debts, Mortgage Liabilities, Liens (Schedule I) (10) _____

11. Total Deductions (total Lines 9 & 10) (11) _____

12. Net Value of Estate (Line 8 minus Line 11) (12) _____

13. Charitable and Governmental Bequests (Schedule J) (13) _____

14. Net Value Subject to Tax (Line 12 minus Line 13) (14) _____

TAX COMPUTATION

15. Spousal Transfers (for dates of death after 6-30-94)
See Instructions for Applicable Percentage on Reverse
Side. (Include values from Schedule K or Schedule M.) (15) _____ x. ___ = _____

16. Amount of Line 14 taxable at 6% rate
(Include values from Schedule K or Schedule M.) (16) _____ x .06 = _____

17. Amount of Line 14 taxable at 15% rate
(Include values from Schedule K or Schedule M.) (17) _____ x .15 = _____

18. Principal tax due (Add tax from Lines 15, 16 and 17.) (18) _____

19. Credits   Spousal Poverty Credit   Prior Payments   Discount   Interest

_____ + _____ + _____ − _____ (19) _____

20. If Line 19 is greater than Line 18, enter the difference on Line 20. This is the **OVERPAYMENT.** (20) _____

A. ☐ **Check here if you are requesting a refund of your overpayment.**

21. If Line 18 is greater than Line 19, enter the difference on Line 21. This is the **TAX DUE.** (21) _____

A. Enter the interest on the balance due on Line 21A. (21A) _____

B. Enter the total of Line 21 and 21A on Line 21B. This is the **BALANCE DUE.** (21B) _____

Make Check Payable to: Register of Wills, Agent

▶▶ **BE SURE TO ANSWER ALL QUESTIONS ON REVERSE SIDE AND TO RECHECK MATH** ◀◀

Under penalties of perjury, I declare that I have examined this return, including accompanying schedules and statements, and to the best of my knowledge and belief, it is true, correct and complete. I declare that all real estate has been reported at true market value. Declaration of preparer other than the personal representative is based on all information of which preparer has any knowledge.

SIGNATURE OF PERSON RESPONSIBLE FOR FILING RETURN   ADDRESS   DATE

SIGNATURE OF PREPARER OTHER THAN REPRESENTATIVE   ADDRESS   DATE

Act #48 of 1994 provides for the reduction of the tax rates imposed on the net value of transfers to or for the use of the spouse. The rates as prescribed by the statute will be:

- 3% (.03) will be applicable for estates of decedents dying on or after 7/1/94 and before 1/1/96

- 2% (.02) will be applicable for estates of decedents dying on or after 1/1/96 and before 1/1/97

- 1% (.01) will be applicable for estates of decedents dying on or after 1/1/97 and before 1/1/98

- Spousal transfers occurring on or after 1/1/98 will be exempt from inheritance tax.

PLEASE ANSWER THE FOLLOWING QUESTIONS
BY PLACING A CHECK MARK (✓) IN THE APPROPRIATE BLOCKS.

	YES	NO
1. Did decedent make a transfer and:		
a. retain the use or income of the property transferred,		
b. retain the right to designate who shall use the property transferred or its income,		
c. retain a reversionary interest; or		
d. receive the promise for life of either payments, benefits or care?		
2. If death occurred on or before December 12, 1982, did decedent within two years preceding death transfer property without receiving adequate consideration? If death occurred after December 12, 1982, did decedent transfer property within one year of death without receiving adequate consideration?		
3. Did decedent own an 'in trust for' bank account at his or her death?		

IF THE ANSWER TO ANY OF THE ABOVE QUESTIONS IS YES,
YOU MUST COMPLETE SCHEDULE G AND FILE IT AS PART OF THE RETURN.

EV-1502 EX+ (12-85)

COMMONWEALTH OF PENNSYLVANIA
INHERITANCE TAX RETURN
RESIDENT DECEDENT

SCHEDULE A
REAL ESTATE

STATE OF _____   FILE NUMBER _____

Property jointly-owned with Right of Survivorship must be disclosed on Schedule F) All real estate should be reported at fair market value which is defined as the price at which property would be exchanged between a willing buyer and a willing seller, neither being compelled to buy or sell, both having reasonable knowledge of the relevant facts.

ITEM NUMBER	DESCRIPTION	VALUE AT DATE OF DEATH
1.		
	TOTAL (Also enter on line 1, Recapitulation)	$

(If more space is needed, insert additional sheets of same size.)

REV-1503 EX+ (4-86)

COMMONWEALTH OF PENNSYLVANIA
INHERITANCE TAX RETURN
RESIDENT DECEDENT

SCHEDULE B
STOCKS AND BONDS

ESTATE OF

FILE NUMBER

(All property jointly-owned with Right of Survivorship must be disclosed on Schedule F.)

ITEM NUMBER	DESCRIPTION	VALUE AT DATE OF DEATH
1.		

| | TOTAL (Also enter on line 2, Recapitulation) | $ |

(If more space is needed, insert additional sheets of same size.)

EV-1504 EX+ (7-83)

COMMONWEALTH OF PENNSYLVANIA
INHERITANCE TAX RETURN
RESIDENT DECEDENT

SCHEDULE "C"
CLOSELY HELD STOCK,
PARTNERSHIP AND PROPRIETORSHIP

ESTATE OF   FILE NUMBER

(Schedule "C-1" or "C-2" must be attached for each business interest of the decedent, other than a proprietorship.)

ITEM NUMBER	DESCRIPTION	VALUE AT DATE OF DEATH
1.		
	TOTAL (Also enter on line 3, Recapitulation)	$

(If more space is needed insert additional sheets of same size)

REV-1505 EX+ (5-88)

COMMONWEALTH OF PENNSYLVANIA
INHERITANCE TAX RETURN
RESIDENT DECEDENT

SCHEDULE C-1
CLOSELY HELD CORPORATE STOCK
INFORMATION REPORT

Please Type or Print

ESTATE OF _____ FILE NUMBER _____

1. Name of Corporation _____ State of Inc. _____

    Street Address_____ Date of Inc. _____

    City _____ State _____ Zip Code _____ Total Number of Shareholders_____

2. Federal I. D. Number _____ Business Reporting Year _____ to _____
    (Same As Federal Form 1120)

3. Type of Business _____ Product _____

4.   5. Estimated Value of Decedent's Interest

STOCK	TYPE	TOTAL # SHARES OUTSTANDING	PAR VALUE	# SHARES OWNED BY DECEDENT	UNIT VALUE	TOTAL
Common						
Preferred						

Provide all rights and restrictions pertaining to each class of stock.

6. Was decedent employed by the Corporation? ☐Yes ☐No

    If yes, Position _____ Annual Salary $_____ Time Devoted to business _____

7. Amount and type of company indebtedness to decedent at date of death: $_____

8. Was there life insurance payable to the corporation upon death of decedent? ☐Yes ☐No

    If yes, Cash Surrender Value: $_____ Net Proceeds Payable: $_____

    Owner of Policy _____

9. Did the decedent sell or transfer stock of this company within one year prior to death if the date of death was on or after 12/13/82 or within two years if the date of death was prior to 12/13/82? ☐ Yes ☐ No

    If yes:

# OF SHARES	TRANSFEREE OR PURCHASER	AMOUNT	DATE

10. Did the corporation have an interest in other corporations or partnerships? ☐Yes ☐No

    If yes, report the necessary information on a separate sheet, including Schedule "C-1" or "C-2" for each interest.

11. Was there a written shareholders' agreement in effect at the time of the decedent's death? ☐Yes ☐No

    If yes, attach copy of agreement.

12. Was the decedent's stock sold? ☐Yes ☐No

    If yes, provide a copy of the agreement of sale, etc.

13. Was the corporation dissolved or liquidated after the decedent's death? ☐Yes ☐No

    If yes, provide a breakdown of liquidation distributions, etc. Attach a separate sheet.

14. Please submit the following information with this schedule:

    A. A detailed description showing the method of computation utilized in the valuation of the decedent's stock.

    B. Complete copies of financial statements or complete copies of the Federal Tax Returns (Federal Form 1120) for the year of death and 4 preceding years.

    C. A statement of dividends paid each year. List those declared and unpaid.

    D. List names of officers, salaries, bonuses and any other benefits received from Corporation.

    E. If the Company owned real estate, submit a list showing the complete address/es and estimated Fair Market Value/s. If Real Estate Appraisals have been secured, please attach copies.

    F. List principal stockholders at date of death, number of shares held, and relationship to decedent.

15. **ALL OTHER INFORMATION RELATIVE TO AFFIXING THE TRUE VALUE OF THE DECEDENT'S INTEREST SHOULD ACCOMPANY THIS SCHEDULE.**

REV-1506 EX+ (5-92)

COMMONWEALTH OF PENNSYLVANIA
INHERITANCE TAX RETURN
RESIDENT DECEDENT

SCHEDULE C-2
PARTNERSHIP
INTEREST REPORT

Please Type or Print

ESTATE OF

FILE NUMBER

The following information must be submitted with this schedule:

A. Detailed description showing the method of computation utilized in the valuation of the decedent's interest.

B. Complete copies of financial statements or complete copies of the Federal Tax Returns (Form 1065) for the year of death and 4 preceding years, including a balance sheet for the year of death.

C. If the Company owned Real Estate, furnish a list showing the complete address/es and estimated Fair Market Value/s. If Real Estate Appraisals have been secured, please attach copies.

D. Any other information relative to the valuation of the decedent's interest.

1. Name of Partnership _____   Federal I. D. Number _____
   (As per Form 1065)

   Address _____   Date Business Commenced _____

   _____   Business Activity _____

2. Decedent was a ☐General ☐Limited partner. If decedent was a limited partner, provide initial investment $_____ .

3.

PARTNER'S NAMES	% OF INCOME	% OF OWNERSHIP	SALARY	BALANCE OF CAPITAL ACCOUNT
A.				
B.				
C.				
D.				

4. Estimated Value of decedent's interest: $_____

5. Was the partnership indebted to the decedent?   ☐Yes   ☐No

   If yes, provide amount of indebtedness $_____.

6. Was there life insurance payable to the partnership upon the death of the decedent? ☐Yes ☐No

   If yes, Cash Surrender Value: $_____ Net proceeds payable: $_____

   Owner of Policy: _____

7. Was there a written partnership agreement in effect at the time of the decedent's death? ☐Yes ☐No
   If yes, attach copy of agreement.

8. Did the partnership have an interest in any other partnerships or corporations? ☐Yes ☐No
   If yes, report the necessary information on a separate sheet, including Schedule "C-1" or "C-2" for each interest.

9. Did the decedent's interest in the partnership change in the year before death if the date of death was on or after 12/13/82 or if death occurred prior to 12/13/82 in the last two years? ☐Yes ☐No

   If yes, explain: _____

10. Was the decedent related to any of the other partners? ☐Yes ☐No

    If yes, explain: _____

11. Was the partnership dissolved or liquidated after decedent's death? ☐Yes ☐No
    If yes, report all the related information, including copies of the Sales Agreement and/or Settlement Sheet.

12. Was the decedent's partnership interest sold? ☐Yes ☐No
    If yes, provide a copy of the agreemnt of sale, etc.

REV-1507 EX+ (7-88)

**COMMONWEALTH OF PENNSYLVANIA
INHERITANCE TAX RETURN
RESIDENT DECEDENT**

SCHEDULE D
MORTGAGES AND NOTES
RECEIVABLE

Please Print or Type

ESTATE OF	FILE NUMBER

(All property jointly-owned with the Right of Survivorship must be disclosed on Schedule F.)

ITEM NUMBER	DESCRIPTION	VALUE AT DATE OF DEATH
	TOTAL (Also enter on line 4, Recapitulation)	$

(If more space is needed, insert additional sheets of same size.)

REV-1508 EX+ (2-87)

COMMONWEALTH OF PENNSYLVANIA
INHERITANCE TAX RETURN
RESIDENT DECEDENT

SCHEDULE E
CASH, BANK DEPOSITS AND MISCELLANEOUS PERSONAL PROPERTY

Please Print or Type

STATE OF

FILE NUMBER

(All property jointly-owned with the Right of Survivorship must be disclosed on Schedule F)

ITEM NUMBER	DESCRIPTION	VALUE AT DATE OF DEATH
	TOTAL (Also enter on line 5, Recapitulation)	$

(Attach additional 8½" x 11" sheets if more space is needed.)

REV-1509 EX+ (12-88)

COMMONWEALTH OF PENNSYLVANIA
INHERITANCE TAX RETURN
RESIDENT DECEDENT

SCHEDULE F
JOINTLY-OWNED PROPERTY

ESTATE OF	FILE NUMBER

Joint tenant(s):

	NAME	ADDRESS	RELATIONSHIP TO DECEDENT
A.			
B.			
C.			

Jointly-owned property:

ITEM NUMBER	LETTER FOR JOINT TENANT	DATE MADE JOINT	DESCRIPTION OF PROPERTY	TOTAL VALUE OF ASSET	DECD'S % INT.	DOLLAR VALUE OF DECEDENT'S INTEREST
1.						
			TOTAL (Also enter on line 6, Recapitulation)			$

(If more space is needed insert additional sheets of same size)

COMMONWEALTH OF PENNSYLVANIA
INHERITANCE TAX RETURN
RESIDENT DECEDENT

SCHEDULE G
TRANSFERS

PLEASE PRINT OR TYPE

ESTATE OF

FILE NUMBER

THIS SCHEDULE MUST BE COMPLETED AND FILED IF THE ANSWER TO ANY OF THE QUESTIONS ON THE REVERSE SIDE OF THE COVER SHEET IS YES.

ITEM NUMBER	DESCRIPTION OF PROPERTY *Include name of the transferee, their relationship to decedent, date of transfer.*	EXCLUSION	TOTAL VALUE OF ASSET	DECD. % INT.	DOLLAR VALUE OF DECEDENT'S INTEREST

TOTAL (Also enter on line 7, Recapitulation) $

(If more space is needed, insert additional sheets of same size.)

REV-1511 EX + (7-88)

COMMONWEALTH OF PENNSYLVANIA
INHERITANCE TAX RETURN
RESIDENT DECEDENT

SCHEDULE H
FUNERAL EXPENSES, ADMINISTRATIVE COSTS AND MISCELLANEOUS EXPENSES

Please Print or Type

ESTATE OF

FILE NUMBER

ITEM NUMBER	DESCRIPTION	AMOUNT
A.	**Funeral Expenses:**	
1.		
B.	**Administrative Costs:**	
1.	Personal Representative Commissions — — Social Security Number of Personal Representative: _____ Year Commissions paid _____	
2.	Attorney Fees	
3.	Family Exemption Claimant _____ Relationship _____ Address of Claimant at decedent's death Street Address _____ City _____ State _____ Zip Code _____	
4.	Probate Fees	
C.	**Miscellaneous Expenses:**	
1.		
2.		
3.		
4.		
5.		
6.		
7.		
8.		
	TOTAL (Also enter on line 9, Recapitulation)	$

(If more space is needed, insert additional sheets of same size.)

REV-1512 EX+ (1-93)

COMMONWEALTH OF PENNSYLVANIA
INHERITANCE TAX RETURN
RESIDENT DECEDENT

SCHEDULE I
DEBTS OF DECEDENT,
MORTGAGE LIABILITIES AND LIENS

Please Print or Type

ESTATE OF

FILE NUMBER

ITEM NUMBER	DESCRIPTION	AMOUNT
1.		
	TOTAL (Also enter on line 10, Recapitulation)	$

(If more space is needed, insert additional sheets of same size.)

REV-1514 EX+ (3-92)

COMMONWEALTH OF PENNSYLVANIA
INHERITANCE TAX RETURN
RESIDENT DECEDENT

SCHEDULE K
LIFE ESTATE/ANNUITY/
TERM CERTAIN

ESTATE OF

FILE NUMBER

This schedule is to be used for all single life, joint or successive life estates and term certain calculations. For dates of death after 12-31-61 and before 5-1-89, actuarial factors for single life calculations can be found in Revenue Booklet (REV-1501B). For dates of death on or after 5-1-89 actuarial factors can be found in IRS Publication # 1457 Actuarial Values, Alpha Volume.

The instrument creating the life interest is a: **(Please attach a copy of instrument)**

☐ Will   ☐ Intervivos Deed of Trust   ☐ Other_____

LIFE ESTATE INTEREST CALCULATION

Name(s) of Life Tenant(s)	Date of Birth	Present Age (Nearest Birthday)	Term of Years Life Estate is Payable
			☐ Life or ☐ Term of Years _____
			☐ Life or ☐ Term of Years _____
			☐ Life or ☐ Term of Years _____
			☐ Life or ☐ Term of Years _____

1. Value of Fund from which Life Estate(s) is payable: .... $_____

2. Actuarial Factor per appropriate Table .... _____
   Interest Table rate - ☐ 3½%   ☐ 6%   ☐ 10%   ☐ Variable Rate _____ %
3. Value of Life Estate (**Line 1 × Line 2**) .... $_____

ANNUITY INTEREST CALCULATION

Name(s) of Annuitant(s)	Date of Birth	Present Age (Nearest Birthday)	Term of Years Annuity is Payable
			☐ Life or ☐ Term of Years _____
			☐ Life or ☐ Term of Years _____
			☐ Life or ☐ Term of Years _____
			☐ Life or ☐ Term of Years _____

1. Value of Fund from which annuity is payable .... $_____
2. Frequency of payout - ☐ Weekly   ☐ Bi-weekly   ☐ Monthly
   ☐ Quarterly   ☐ Semi-Annually   ☐ Annually   ☐ Other _____   _____

3. Amount of payout per period.. _____

4. Annual payment .... _____
5. Annuity Factor (see instructions)
   Interest Table rate - ☐ 3½%   ☐ 6%   ☐ 10%   ☐ Variable Rate _____ %   _____

6. Adjustment Factor (see instructions) .... _____
7. Value of Annuity - If using 3½%, 6%, 10% or if variable rate and period payout is at end of period, calculation is: **Line 4 × Line 5 × Line 6** .... _____
   If using variable rate and period payout is at beginning of period, calculation is:
   (Line 4 × Line 5 × Line 6) + Line 3.

NOTE: The values of the funds which create the above future interests must be reported as part of the Estate Assets, Line 1 through Line 7. The Resulting Life/Annuity Interest(s) should be reported at the appropriate tax rate on Lines 13, 15 and 16 as required.

REV-1645 EX+ (7-85)

COMMONWEALTH OF PENNSYLVANIA
INHERITANCE TAX RETURN
RESIDENT DECEDENT

INHERITANCE TAX
SCHEDULE L-1
REMAINDER PREPAYMENT ELECTION
-ASSETS-

FILE NUMBER _____

I.	Estate of		
	(Last Name)	(First Name)	(Middle Initial)

II.	Item No.	Description	Value
		A. Real Estate (please describe)	
		Total value of real estate (include on Section II, Line C-1 on Schedule L)	$
		B. Stocks and Bonds (please list)	
		Total value of stocks and bonds (include on Section II, Line C-2 on Schedule L)	$
		C. Closely Held Stock/Partnership (attach Schedule C-1 and/or C-2) (please list)	
		Total value of Closely Held/Partnership (include on Section II, Line C-3 on Schedule L)	$
		D. Mortgages and Notes (please list)	
		Total value of Mortgages and Notes (include on Section II, Line C-4 on Schedule L)	$
		E. Cash and Miscellaneous Personal Property (please list)	
		Total value of Cash/Misc. Pers. Property (include on Section II, Line C-5 on Schedule L)	$
III.		TOTAL (Also enter on Section II, Line C-6 on Schedule L)	$

(If more space is needed, attach additional 8½ x 11 sheets.)

INHERITANCE TAX
SCHEDULE M

FUTURE INTEREST COMPROMISE

FILE NUMBER _____

I. **Estate of** _____

(Last Name)　　　　　　　　(First Name)　　　　(Middle Initial)

This schedule is appropriate only for Estates of decedents dying after December 12, 1982.

This schedule is to be used for all future interests where the rate of tax which will be applicable when the future interest vests in possession and enjoyment cannot be established with certainty.

II. **Beneficiaries**

NAME OF BENEFICIARY	RELATIONSHIP	SEX (M) Male (F) Female	DATE OF BIRTH	AGE ON DATE OF DECEDENT'S DEATH
1.				
2.				
3.				
4.				
5.				

III. **Explanation of Compromise Offer:**

IV. **Summary of Compromise Offer:**

1. Value of Future Interest: . . . . $_____

2. Amount of Line 1 Exempt from Tax . . . . $_____
   (also enter on Line 13, Recapitulation)

3. Amount of Line 1 Taxable at 6% Rate . . . . $_____
   (also enter on Line 15, Tax Computation)

4. Amount of Line 1 Taxable at 15% Rate . . . . $_____
   (also enter on Line 16, Tax Computation)

(If more space is needed, attach additional 8½ x 11" sheets)

REV-1649 EX+ (8/95)

COMMONWEALTH OF PENNSYLVANIA

INHERITANCE TAX RETURN

RESIDENT DECEDENT

SCHEDULE O
TRANSFERS TO SURVIVING SPOUSE

ESTATE OF   **FileNumber**

PART A: Enter the description and value of all interests, both taxable and non-taxable, regardless of location, (net of deductions) which pass to the decedent's surviving spouse by will, intestacy, operation of law, or otherwise.

Description of items	Amount
1	

Part A Total: Enter the amount shown on the recapitulation sheet in the Decedent Information Section.

Election To Subject Property To Tax Under Section 2113(A) As A Taxable Transfer By This Decedent.

If a trust or similar arrangement meets the requirements of Section 2113(A), and:

    a. The trust or similar arrangement is listed on Schedule O, and

    b. The value of the trust or similar arrangement is entered in whole or in part as an asset on Schedule O,

then the transferor's personal representative may specifically identify the trust (all or a fractional portion or percentage) to be included in the election to have such trust or similar property treated as a taxable transfer in this estate. If less than the entire value of the trust or similar property is included as a taxable transfer on Schedule O, the personal representative shall be considered to have made the election only as to a fraction of the trust or similar arrangement. The numerator of this fraction is equal to the amount of the trust or similar arrangement included as a taxable asset on Schedule O. The denominator is equal to the total value of the trust or similar arrangement.

ELECTION: Do you elect under Section 2113(A) to treat as a taxable transfer in this estate all or a portion of a trust or similar arrangement

    created for the sole use of this decedent's surviving spouse during the surviving spouse's entire lifetime?

    YES [ ]   **NO** [ ]   Signature_____ Date _____

Note: If the election applies to more than one trust or similar arrangement, then a separate form must be signed and filed.

Part B: Enter the description and value of all interests, both taxable and non-taxable, regardless of location, (net of deductions)
which pass to the decedent's surviving spouse for which a Section 2113 (A) election is being made.

Description of items	Amount
1	

Part B Total

APPENDIX 27

Letter to Register of Wills

A letter similar to this may be used to forward the tax return, inventory, affidavit and status report along with payment of the inheritance tax.

LETTER TO REGISTER OF WILLS

LETTERHEAD

Date

Name
Register of Wills Office
_____ County Court House
address

Re: Estate of _____, Deceased
             #_____

Dear Mr. _____:

       With this letter I enclose the Inheritance Tax Return, Inventory, Affidavit Re Personal Property Tax and Status Report for the above captioned estate together with check in the amount of $_____ in payment of the State Transfer Inheritance Tax. Please issue your receipt for the payment of the tax.

                                        Very truly yours,

                                        _____(signature)
                                        (typed name)
                                        Executor

APPENDIX 28

Commonwealth of Pennsylvania Receipt for Inheritance and Estate Tax

This form is self-explanatory.

1 NO. M448154 **COMMONWEALTH OF PENNSYLVANIA**
DEPARTMENT OF REVENUE
OFFICIAL RECEIPT ● PENNSYLVANIA INHERITANCE AND ESTATE TAX
REV-1162 EX (17-80)

RECEIVED FROM:

Edmund Jones, Esquire
P.O. Box 566
Media, PA 19063

HERE

7 ACN ASSESSMENT CONTROL NUMBER	**8** AMOUNT
101	-
	FOLD

ESTATE INFORMATION:

2 FILE NUMBER

3 NAME OF DECEDENT (LAST) (FIRST) (MI)

4 DATE OF PAYMENT
5/1/89

5 POSTMARK DATE
5/1/89 H.D.

COUNTY
Delaware

DATE OF DEATH
4/28/87

REMARKS

SEAL

6 TOTAL AMOUNT PAID _____

RECEIVED BY *Elizabeth M. Brennan*
SIGNATURE

TAXPAYER Elizabeth M. Brennan, Chief Deputy

APPENDIX 29

Form 706, United States Estate Tax Return

This form has 41 pages and is rather overwhelming at first glance. The first three pages are reproduced here to indicate the requirements levied on the administrator or executor for reporting and the need for accurate record keeping from day one in order to complete the return. Page three has a recap of the schedules required as a part of the return. The return is due nine months after date of death. It is likely that the attorney for the estate will be called upon to complete this return - at least that was true for those estates in which I was involved.

Form **706**

(Rev. August 1993)

Department of the Treasury
Internal Revenue Service

United States Estate (and Generation-Skipping Transfer) Tax Return

Estate of a citizen or resident of the United States (see separate instructions). To be
filed for decedents dying after October 8, 1990. For Paperwork Reduction Act Notice,
see page 1 of the instructions.

OMB No. 1545-0015
Expires 12-31-95

Part 1.—Decedent and Executor

1a Decedent's first name and middle initial (and maiden name, if any)	1b Decedent's last name	2 Decedent's social security no.

3a Domicile at time of death (county and state, or foreign country)	3b Year domicile established	4 Date of birth	5 Date of death

6a Name of executor (see instructions)	6b Executor's address (number and street including apartment or suite no. or rural route; city, town, or post office; state; and ZIP code)

6c Executor's social security number (see instructions)

7a Name and location of court where will was probated or estate administered	7b Case number

8 If decedent died testate, check here ▶ ☐ and attach a certified copy of the will. **9** If Form 4768 is attached, check here ▶ ☐

10 If Schedule R-1 is attached, check here ▶ ☐

Part 2.—Tax Computation

1	Total gross estate (from Part 5, Recapitulation, page 3, item 10)	**1**	
2	Total allowable deductions (from Part 5, Recapitulation, page 3, item 20)	**2**	
3	Taxable estate (subtract line 2 from line 1)	**3**	
4	Adjusted taxable gifts (total taxable gifts (within the meaning of section 2503) made by the decedent after December 31, 1976, other than gifts that are includible in decedent's gross estate (section 2001(b))	**4**	
5	Add lines 3 and 4	**5**	
6	Tentative tax on the amount on line 5 from Table A in the instructions	**6**	
7a	If line 5 exceeds $10,000,000, enter the lesser of line 5 or $21,040,000. If line 5 is $10,000,000 or less, skip lines 7a and 7b and enter -0- on line 7c . **7a**		
b	Subtract $10,000,000 from line 7a **7b**		
c	Enter 5% (.05) of line 7b	**7c**	
8	Total tentative tax (add lines 6 and 7c)	**8**	
9	Total gift tax payable with respect to gifts made by the decedent after December 31, 1976. Include gift taxes by the decedent's spouse for such spouse's share of split gifts (section 2513) only if the decedent was the donor of these gifts and they are includible in the decedent's gross estate (see instructions)	**9**	
10	Gross estate tax (subtract line 9 from line 8)	**10**	
11	Maximum unified credit against estate tax **11** 192,800 00		
12	Adjustment to unified credit. (This adjustment may not exceed $6,000. See page 6 of the instructions.) **12**		
13	Allowable unified credit (subtract line 12 from line 11).	**13**	
14	Subtract line 13 from line 10 (but do not enter less than zero)	**14**	
15	Credit for state death taxes. Do not enter more than line 14. Compute the credit by using the amount on line 3 less $60,000. See Table B in the instructions and **attach credit evidence** (see instructions)	**15**	
16	Subtract line 15 from line 14	**16**	
17	Credit for Federal gift taxes on pre-1977 gifts (section 2012) (attach computation) **17**		
18	Credit for foreign death taxes (from Schedule(s) P). (Attach Form(s) 706CE) **18**		
19	Credit for tax on prior transfers (from Schedule Q) **19**		
20	Total (add lines 17, 18, and 19)	**20**	
21	Net estate tax (subtract line 20 from line 16)	**21**	
22	Generation-skipping transfer taxes (from Schedule R, Part 2, line 10) . .	**22**	
23	Section 4980A increased estate tax (from Schedule S, Part I, line 17) (see instructions)	**23**	
24	Total transfer taxes (add lines 21, 22, and 23)	**24**	
25	Prior payments. Explain in an attached statement **25**		
26	United States Treasury bonds redeemed in payment of estate tax . **26**		
27	Total (add lines 25 and 26).	**27**	
28	Balance due (or overpayment) (subtract line 27 from line 24).	**28**	

Under penalties of perjury, I declare that I have examined this return, including accompanying schedules and statements, and to the best of my knowledge and belief, it is true, correct, and complete. Declaration of preparer other than the executor is based on all information of which preparer has any knowledge.

Signature(s) of executor(s)

Date

Signature of preparer other than executor

Address (and ZIP code)

Date

Cat. No. 20548R

Estate of:

Part 3.—Elections by the Executor

Please check the "Yes" or "No" box for each question.

		Yes	No
1	Do you elect alternate valuation?		
2	Do you elect special use valuation? If "Yes," you must complete and attach Schedule A–1		
3	Do you elect to pay the taxes in installments as described in section 6166? . . . . If "Yes," you must attach the additional information described in the instructions.		
4	Do you elect to postpone the part of the taxes attributable to a reversionary or remainder interest as described in section 6163?		

Part 4.—General Information (Note: *Please attach the necessary supplemental documents.* **You must attach the death certificate.**)

Authorization to receive confidential tax information under Regulations section 601.504(b)(2)(i), to act as the estate's representative before the Internal Revenue Service, and to make written or oral presentations on behalf of the estate if return prepared by an attorney, accountant, or enrolled agent for the executor:

Name of representative (print or type)	State	Address (number, street, and room or suite no., city, state, and ZIP code)

I declare that I am the ☐ attorney/ ☐ certified public accountant/ ☐ enrolled agent (you must check the applicable box) for the executor and prepared this return for the executor. I am not under suspension or disbarment from practice before the Internal Revenue Service and am qualified to practice in the state shown above.

Signature	CAF number	Date	Telephone number

1 Death certificate number and issuing authority (attach a copy of the death certificate to this return).

2 Decedent's business or occupation. If retired, check here ► ☐ and state decedent's former business or occupation.

3 Marital status of the decedent at time of death:

☐ Married

☐ Widow or widower—Name, SSN, and date of death of deceased spouse ► ....

....

☐ Single

☐ Legally separated

☐ Divorced—Date divorce decree became final ►

4a Surviving spouse's name	4b Social security number	4c Amount received (see instructions)

5 Individuals (other than the surviving spouse), trusts, or other estates who receive benefits from the estate (do not include charitable beneficiaries shown in Schedule O) (see instructions). For Privacy Act Notice (applicable to individual beneficiaries only), see the Instructions for Form 1040.

Name of individual, trust, or estate receiving $5,000 or more	Identifying number	Relationship to decedent	Amount (see instructions)

All unascertainable beneficiaries and those who receive less than $5,000 . . . . ►	
Total	

(Continued on next page)

Part 4.—General Information (continued)

	Please check the "Yes" or "No" box for each question.	Yes	No
6	Does the gross estate contain any section 2044 property (qualified terminable interest property (QTIP) from a prior gift or estate) (see page 5 of the instructions)?		
7a	Have Federal gift tax returns ever been filed?		
	If "Yes," please attach copies of the returns, if available, and furnish the following information:		

7b Period(s) covered	7c Internal Revenue office(s) where filed

If you answer "Yes" to any of questions 8–16, you must attach additional information as described in the instructions.

		Yes	No
8a	Was there any insurance on the decedent's life that is not included on the return as part of the gross estate?		
b	Did the decedent own any insurance on the life of another that is not included in the gross estate?		
9	Did the decedent at the time of death own any property as a joint tenant with right of survivorship in which (a) one or more of the other joint tenants was someone other than the decedent's spouse, and (b) less than the full value of the property is included on the return as part of the gross estate? If "Yes," you must complete and attach Schedule E		
10	Did the decedent, at the time of death, own any interest in a partnership or unincorporated business or any stock in an inactive or closely held corporation?		
11	Did the decedent make any transfer described in section 2035, 2036, 2037, or 2038 (see the instructions for Schedule G)? If "Yes," you must complete and attach Schedule G		
12	Were there in existence at the time of the decedent's death:		
a	Any trusts created by the decedent during his or her lifetime?		
b	Any trusts not created by the decedent under which the decedent possessed any power, beneficial interest, or trusteeship?		
13	Did the decedent ever possess, exercise, or release any general power of appointment? If "Yes," you must complete and attach Schedule H		
14	Was the marital deduction computed under the transitional rule of Public Law 97-34, section 403(e)(3) (Economic Recovery Tax Act of 1981)?		
	If "Yes," attach a separate computation of the marital deduction, enter the amount on item 18 of the Recapitulation, and note on item 18 "computation attached."		
15	Was the decedent, immediately before death, receiving an annuity described in the "General" paragraph of the instructions for Schedule I? If "Yes," you must complete and attach Schedule I		
16	Did the decedent have a total "excess retirement accumulation" (as defined in section 4980A(d)) in qualified employer plans and individual retirement plans? If "Yes," you must complete and attach Schedule S		

Part 5.—Recapitulation

Item number	Gross estate	Alternate value	Value at date of death
1	Schedule A—Real Estate		
2	Schedule B—Stocks and Bonds		
3	Schedule C—Mortgages, Notes, and Cash		
4	Schedule D—Insurance on the Decedent's Life (attach Form(s) 712)		
5	Schedule E—Jointly Owned Property (attach Form(s) 712 for life insurance)		
6	Schedule F—Other Miscellaneous Property (attach Form(s) 712 for life insurance)		
7	Schedule G—Transfers During Decedent's Life (attach Form(s) 712 for life insurance)		
8	Schedule H—Powers of Appointment		
9	Schedule I—Annuities		
10	Total gross estate (add items 1 through 9). Enter here and on line 1 of the Tax Computation		

Item number	Deductions	Amount
11	Schedule J—Funeral Expenses and Expenses Incurred in Administering Property Subject to Claims	
12	Schedule K—Debts of the Decedent	
13	Schedule K—Mortgages and Liens	
14	Total of items 11 through 13	
15	Allowable amount of deductions from item 14 (see the instructions for item 15 of the Recapitulation)	
16	Schedule L—Net Losses During Administration	
17	Schedule L—Expenses Incurred in Administering Property Not Subject to Claims	
18	Schedule M—Bequests, etc., to Surviving Spouse	
19	Schedule O—Charitable, Public, and Similar Gifts and Bequests	
20	Total allowable deductions (add items 15 through 19). Enter here and on line 2 of the Tax Computation	

BOOK ORDER FORM

FAX Orders: 610 544 6199

POSTAL Orders: Edgewood Publishing Company
F. William Bauers, Jr.
P.O. Box 201
Swarthmore, PA 19081

Please send the following books:

Number	Title	Unit Cost	Total
	Where There's A Will ...	$29.95	$
	*Sales Tax - PA 6 %		
	Shipping ($4.00 first book; $2.00 for each additional book)		
	TOTAL		$

Send To:

Company _____

Name _____

Address _____

City _____ **State** _____ **Zip** _____

Telephone _____

Please include payment by check or money order

* Add 6 % sales tax for books shipped to Pennsylvania address

BOOK ORDER FORM

FAX Orders: 610 544 6199

POSTAL Orders: Edgewood Publishing Company
F. William Bauers, Jr.
P.O. Box 201
Swarthmore, PA 19081

Please send the following books:

Number	Title	Unit Cost	Total
	Where There's A Will ...	$29.95	$
	*Sales Tax - PA 6 %		
	Shipping ($4.00 first book; $2.00 for each additional book)		
	TOTAL		$

Send To:

Company _____

Name _____

Address _____

City _____ State_____ Zip_____

Telephone _____

Please include payment by check or money order

* Add 6 % sales tax for books shipped to Pennsylvania address